Praise for *The Stuff of Heroes*

"In early works, Dr. Cohen demonstrated how military leadership principles could be applied to all organizations. In this book he goes to the next level by examining not just what was successful for any given military leader, but what traits and actions provided the foundation for that success . . . this book should have a lasting impact."

—**General Ronald Fogelman, former Chief of Staff, U.S. Air Force**

"A first-class primer on the elusive subject of leadership, punctuated with stirring examples from both the military and civilian worlds."

—**General H. Norman Schwarzkopf, U.S. Army, Ret.**

"A must-read by aspiring leaders in and out of uniform."

—**General Alexander Haig Jr., former Supreme Allied Commander, Europe, and U.S. Secretary of State**

"Following one of his own universal rules, Dr. Cohen absolutely knows his stuff. If you want to know how to lead any organization, read this book."

—**Barry Gordon, past president, Screen Actors Guild**

"Cohen casts a wide net—back through time and across many disciplines. He has found the secret of what makes great leaders do great things."

—**Ernest Micek, CEO, Gargill, Inc.**

"Not only does this book have good stuff, it has the RIGHT STUFF!"

—**Colonel Frank Borman, former astronaut and CEO of Eastern Airlines**

"Professor Cohen's 'Eight Universal Laws' are not presented in bloodless abstract, but are instead revealed through examples of real people being tested."
   —**Robert A. Lutz, vice chairman, Chrysler Corporation**

"This is not just 'the stuff of heroes.' It is the stuff of all leaders for the millennium."
   —**Phillip Rooney, vice chairman, the ServiceMaster Company**

"There is a tremendous amount of value to this book, especially for the young generations of leaders who have not experienced military service or learned leadership lessons through the 'scars of battle.'"
   —**Jeffrey M. Schmidt, president, Schmidt-Cannon International**

Praise for *The Art of the Leader* and *The New Art of the Leader*

"A valuable reference for industry and for all leaders. I wish I had read it when I was a staff sergeant about to become an armored division second lieutenant. As a matter of fact, I wish I had been able to study it as I moved up the ranks through general, and especially when I became a Fortune 500 corporate officer."

— **Lt. General W. D. Johnson, U.S. Air Force, Ret.; corporate vice president, Baxter International; and former Chief of Staff, Strategic Air Command, and director, Defense Nuclear Agency**

"Dr. Cohen's book makes a significant contribution to the art of leadership . . . I recommend it to all interested in leadership."

— **Admiral Elmo R. Zumwalt Jr., U.S. Navy, Ret., former Chief of Naval Operations**

"I have grave doubts that leadership can be taught, but it can be developed. If you don't get started right with basic honesty, you won't be much of a leader. If you have what it takes, Dr. Cohen's book is very, very well done and can help."

— **Senator Barry Goldwater, former senator from Arizona**

"The range of sources and examples in *The Art of the Leader* is most impressive. Leadership skills can be taught and developed in those who possess that nascent quality. Dr. Cohen's book not only proves it, but contributes to the process."

— **John D. Ong, chairman of the board, BFGoodrich Company**

"Bill Cohen knows more about what makes great leaders than anyone I know."

— **General Frederick Kroesen, former Commander, U.S. Army Europe**

"A most interesting and illuminating book; it will be particularly useful to anyone striving to strengthen his leadership abilities."
> —General Andrew J. Goodpaster, U.S. Army, Ret.; chairman, the Atlantic Council of the United States; former Supreme Allied Commander, Europe; and 51st Superintendent, United States Military Academy

"Full of excellent examples and analogies—crisp and clear. Well done!"
> —Frank Popoff, president and CEO, the Dow Chemical Company

"Easy reading, good logic, and a novel approach. It will deservedly attract a wide range of readers."
> —James Wood, chairman and CEO, the Great Atlantic and Pacific Tea Company, Inc.

"Leaders aren't born that way, but they do need to learn the techniques which Bill Cohen has vividly explained in his book."
> —Mary Kay Ash, chairman, Mary Kay Cosmetics

HEROIC LEADERSHIP

LEADING WITH INTEGRITY AND HONOR

William A. Cohen

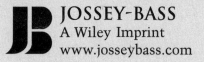

JOSSEY-BASS
A Wiley Imprint
www.josseybass.com

Published by Jossey-Bass
A Wiley Imprint
989 Market Street, San Francisco, CA 94103-1741—www.josseybass.com

Jossey-Bass books and products are available through most bookstores. To contact Jossey-Bass directly call our Customer Care Department within the U.S. at 800-956-7739, outside the U.S. at 317-572-3986, or fax 317-572-4002.

Jossey-Bass also publishes its books in a variety of electronic formats. Some content that appears in print may not be available in electronic books.

Library of Congress Cataloging-in-Publication Data

Cohen, William A.
    Heroic leadership : leading with integrity and honor / William A. Cohen.
      p. cm.
    Includes bibliographical references and index.
    ISBN 978-0-470-40501-7 (cloth)
      1. Leadership.   2. Employee motivation.   I. Title.
    HD57.7.C6427 2010
    658.4'092—dc22

                                     2010004758

Printed in the United States of America
FIRST EDITION
HB Printing   10 9 8 7 6 5 4 3 2 1

To the members of the U.S. Armed Forces
of every branch of service,
who have performed incredible feats of courage and leadership
and inspired and assisted me in learning how to
"beat swords into plowshares"

CONTENTS

· ·

Part Three • The Eight Competencies of Heroic Leadership 159

INTRODUCTION

• •

The Concept of Heroic Leadership

• •

In the spring of 2009, I attended the fiftieth reunion of my graduation from the United States Military Academy at West Point. I was seated next to my classmate Harry Walters. As a cadet Harry Walters had been an outstanding athlete, a fullback in Army's undefeated 1958 season. At the end of the year the team had ranked third in national standings, and another classmate, Pete Dawkins, had won the Heisman Trophy. Harry had gone on to serve honorably in the Army, become CEO of a corporation, and under President Reagan had served as Assistant Secretary of the Army and then Veterans Affairs Administrator.

However, the school that had once fielded great football teams and produced outstanding athletes like Walters and Dawkins has done poorly in football for a number of years, even though its sister service academies, Navy and Air Force, have done pretty well during the same period. I asked Harry what he thought the problem was. Were we not getting the same quality of players as our sister academies? Were we expecting too much from them in meeting West Point standards in academics and leadership while looking for great things on the gridiron? Without hesitation, Harry answered, "There is no doubt at all about the problem. It is always the coach, not the players and other issues which makes success at football tougher for the players. When Red Blaik coached, Army won. It is always the leader, and in football, that is the coach. When we once again start winning, it will be because of the coach."

I instantly realized that Harry was 100 percent correct. Successful coaches practice *Heroic Leadership*. Heroic Leadership is special. It requires leading a group with absolute integrity while raising individual performance to a personal best and building a team spirit of sacrifice for the common good. Heroic Leadership requires tough standards. Meeting them may sound like an impossible dream, something rarely if ever achieved. However, it is not. Heroic Leadership does exist and it has left clues—descriptions, names, and dates—everything we need to emulate and duplicate such "impossible" successes in our own organizations. These successes are never more looked for than when we are in the grip of a severe recession, or when our organization is in trouble for any cause. It makes no difference whether your organization is a corporation, a nonprofit, a school, or an athletic team: Heroic Leadership is crucial.

Peter F. Drucker, the greatest management thinker of our time, knew Heroic Leadership and promoted it throughout his long career and in his thirty-nine books and hundreds of articles. In his first book devoted specifically to management, Drucker wrote that the first systematic book on leadership, written more than two thousand years earlier, was still the best. Its author, Xenophon, was a Greek general, and he wrote on leadership in battle. Years later Drucker said, "The Army trains and develops more leaders than do all other institutions together—and with a lower casualty rate." A few years ago Richard Cavanaugh, president and CEO of the Conference Board, wrote about a meeting he conducted at which both Drucker and legendary CEO Jack Welch were cospeakers.

They were asked, who does the best job of developing leaders? To quote Cavanaugh, "To my surprise, the usual suspects so often cited for finding and training leaders didn't figure—not the Harvard Business School, or Goldman Sachs, or McKinsey & Company, or General Electric, or IBM, or Procter & Gamble. The enthusiastic choice of both of these management legends was the United States military."

Battle Leadership

War is one of mankind's least commendable activities. The misery, death, and destruction that war causes are so horrendous that even professional soldiers publicly condemn it and seek to avoid it. Even "just wars"—wars that might be counted as having a positive outcome—are unbelievably costly. Ending slavery in the United States cost almost a million casualties at a time when the total U.S. population, North and South, was only a little over thirty-one million. Getting rid of the scourge of Nazism and fascism cost the world fifty-six million casualties. Despite these grim facts, war has been with us almost constantly. Within a span of over seven thousand years of recorded history, historians have found fewer than one hundred *days* in which man was not engaged in warfare somewhere in the world.

Mankind was forced to learn about leadership under the most trying of conditions. As General George S. Patton said, "Wars may be fought with weapons, but they are won by men." Men and women must be led. Experience gained on thousands of battlefields has developed and fine-tuned the abilities of combat leaders and given them practical knowledge that collectively far surpasses that of nonmilitary organizations. Little wonder that Peter Drucker, the "Father of Modern Management," discovered that battle leadership taught two millennia ago was absolutely compelling for modern business and nonprofit organizations.

In battle leadership life-and-death decisions must be made in an environment rarely faced by the noncombat leader. In that environment there is:

- The prospect of horrific and far-reaching effects on the combat unit and those it represents
- Personal danger
- Food and sleep deprivation
- Physical hazards
- Constant stress
- The need to make critical decisions rapidly and with incomplete and unconfirmed information
- The potential requirement of having to assume far greater responsibility with little preparation or warning

Battle leadership is a type of Heroic Leadership, but it is possibly the only leadership environment where both leaders and those being led would prefer to be somewhere else. Yet before you simply assume that battle leaders are brutes and that Heroic Leadership is something automatic, mindless, and not worth your time, you'd better think again.

The Carrot and the Stick

It is true that "carrot and stick" leadership has been practiced on the battlefield and in the boardroom, and still is at times. It does have its time and place, but contrary to common belief the term is not synonymous with military leadership. In Drucker's favorite leadership book, Xenophon describes the limitations of carrot-and-stick leadership: Cyrus the Great of Persia was an absolute monarch. He held the power of life and death over his followers. He could reward or punish and motivate in any way he chose. Cyrus's father asked him what he thought was the best way to motivate his followers. Cyrus answered, "After reflecting about these things, I think I see in all of them that which especially incites to obedience is the praising and honoring of one who obeys and the dishonoring of the one who disobeys."

There it is: carrot-and-stick leadership, described more than two thousand years ago. Cyrus's father agreed that this approach sometimes worked. "However," he continued, "when people think that they may incur harm in obeying, they are not so ready to respond to the threat of punishments or to be seduced by gifts." Then he told Cyrus of a far superior way to induce human beings to obey, even when danger was present. The leader had only to take care of his subordinates better than they could take care of themselves, and to do so even before looking after his own interests. There is an old injunction in the military that a commander must not eat until the soldiers eat first. That's Heroic Leadership, and it will work in any organization.

How to Acquire Heroic Leadership

I've spent almost thirty years immersed in the research for this book. That research is about acquiring the imagination to understand and apply the lessons of Heroic Leadership to corporations, nonprofit organizations, and government. Without question, an understanding of such lessons and our ability to apply them are desperately needed now. This is a time of great challenge, which threatens the very fabric of society. We face not only the greatest financial crisis of our time but a worldwide crisis of extremism and threats to our way of life—indeed, to our very lives.

Much of this book is based on concepts developed in three of my earlier books, now out of print: *The Art of the Leader*, *The Stuff of Heroes: The Eight Universal Laws of Leadership*, and *The New Art of the Leader*. This book is divided into three parts. The first part is based on research I conducted with more than two hundred combat leaders from all branches of the military, and of many ranks, who after leaving the military went on to very successful careers in civilian life. I call this part "The Eight Universal Laws of Heroic Leadership." Obeying these laws gives you the correct over-all approach to implementing Heroic Leadership no matter your field of application or the environment or particular challenges you may face as a leader. The second part is "The Eight Basic Influence Tools." Of course an infinite number of tools may be used to influence others—but these are the basics. Master these, and you will be able to apply the eight laws to specific challenges you may face. Finally, Part Three presents "The Eight Competencies of Heroic Leadership." Here again, many competencies are useful in applying the concepts of Heroic Leadership, but these I found to be most often applied by successful Heroic Leaders.

Throughout the book you will find

- Real-world examples from business as well as battle, chosen to give you the knowledge and confidence to lead in any situation you may confront, whether lead-ing a company, an army, or even a country

- Proven strategies and results-oriented techniques to apply the principles of Heroic Leadership and multiply the productivity of any group or organization

- New ideas for motivating people and helping them achieve new heights of personal and group performance

- Little-known but highly effective methods for building teamwork and esprit de corps

- Methods for developing yourself as a leader and reach-ing your full potential

- Strategies used by combat leaders to accomplish goals others thought impossible

This is not a "business is war" book. Your challenge is not to turn your organization into a combat-ready military unit. Rather it is to apply the principles of Heroic Leadership to your own organization and allow it to do what I have found leaders of the heroic mold to do: dare the impossible and achieve the extraordinary.

PART ONE

The Eight Universal Laws of Heroic Leadership

In combat, life is hard: terrible hazards, lousy working conditions, great uncertainty. Nonetheless, battle leaders achieve amazing results by following these eight principles:

- Maintain absolute integrity.
- Know your stuff.
- Declare your expectations.
- Show uncommon commitment.
- Expect positive results.
- Take care of your people.
- Put duty before self.
- Get out in front.

These principles work in civilian life as well as in combat. Whether you are the CEO of a major corporation or the coach of a kids' ball team, they are the foundation of Heroic Leadership.

CHAPTER 1

• •

Maintain Absolute
Integrity

• •

What quality is most universally prized among those who lead others under demanding circumstances in combat, or in business? In simple terms, it's integrity: adherence to a set of values that incorporate honesty and freedom from deception. But integrity is more than honesty. It means doing the right thing regardless of circumstances or inconvenience to the leader or the organization. Our leaders and teachers sometimes waver, as General Colin Powell (who fought there) says of Vietnam: "Our senior officers knew the war was going badly. Yet they bowed to groupthink pressure and kept up pretenses, the phony measure of body counts, the comforting illusion of secure hamlets, the inflated progress reports. As a corporate entity, the military failed to talk straight to its political superiors or to itself."[1]

Far better that they and we listen to men of integrity such as Thomas Jefferson, who gave the following warning: "He who permits himself to tell a lie often finds it much easier to do it a second and third time, till at length it becomes habitual; he tells lies without attending to it, and truths without the world believing him.

This falsehood of the tongue leads to that of the heart, and in time depraves all its good dispositions."[2]

• • • •

Major Clay McCutchan was an air commando and pilot of an AC-130 gunship in the Air Force Reserve. Extensively modified with side-firing guns and the latest acquisition electronics, the AC-130 was a formidable aircraft. It could loiter for long periods of time until needed. When called upon, it could provide unparalleled firepower to destroy most targets in areas where the ground defenses were not too heavy.

In December 1989, McCutchan and his crew were one of two Air Force Reserve crews who volunteered to relieve an active duty AC-130 crew assigned to Panama during the Christmas holidays. They had done this three times before. What McCutchan and others didn't know was that the decision to invade Panama and capture dictator Manuel Noriega had been made a few days earlier by President Ronald Reagan. The invasion, called Operation Just Cause, was set to begin the night of December 19, 1989, only two days after McCutchan's arrival.

The objectives of Operation Just Cause were to capture Noriega and return him to the United States to stand trial on drug charges. The Air Commandos—or Air Force Special Operations, as it was now called—were to spearhead the invasion. Active-duty gunship crews had practiced for months at firing at and destroying mock-ups of certain predesignated targets. Since McCutchan's crew had not participated in this training, they were given a different mission. His crew was put on standby alert to guard Howard Air Force Base in the Canal Zone and the Panama Canal itself, in case it came under attack.

When no attack against the base came, they were ordered into the air to respond, if called upon, to help friendly troops fighting on the ground. For some time they flew around without a specific assignment. At length they were sent to another airfield to aid a group of civilians who had been immobilized by a sniper. A few rounds from their 40mm guns took care of that problem. Again they flew around, waiting for a new job. Finally, McCutchan and his crew were ordered to attack three enemy armored cars along the Fort Amador Causeway. They made radio contact with the Forward Air Controller (FAC) on the ground right away. (The FAC's job is to control all friendly air strikes in his assigned area.) After they had located the armored cars, the controller told them, "You're cleared to take them out."

As McCutchan prepared to fire, his sensor operator and fire-control officer (FCO) spotted thirty to forty troops coming out of the jungle. The FCO called the controller on the ground and told him about the arrival of these new forces. "Take them out too; they're not ours," said the controller. In the AC-130A that McCutchan flew, the pilot fired the guns using a thumb trigger. As his thumb began to itch in readiness, his crew studied the situation closely using special sensors.[3] The more they looked, the more convinced they became that these new troops were Americans. McCutchan had just positioned his airplane for the attack, when one of his crew stopped him: "Don't fire, they may be friendly!"

McCutchan took his thumb off the trigger. After talking it over with his crew, he called the FAC on the ground again and told him that they had identified the troops with the vehicles as possibly American.

"Negative, negative, they are not friendlies. They are enemy, and you are cleared to fire," the controller responded, the frustration clear in his voice. By now the FAC was excited. "Shoot, shoot, shoot," he intoned.

McCutchan called his command post back at Howard Air Force Base and briefed them on the situation. He asked for positive confirmation before firing. After several minutes the command post duty officer came back with a decision. "These are confirmed enemy. You are ordered to fire."

Now McCutchan's actions were no longer discretionary. He had been given a direct order. He had also been given the supreme test of integrity. He and his crew believed that the troops near the enemy vehicles were friendly. Usually the FAC on the ground had a much better picture of what was going on. But with the AC-130's sophisticated equipment, the crew might be in a better position to judge whether the troops were friendlies or enemies. "Our forces were not being fired on by these vehicles or these troops, and they were not an immediate threat to anyone," reasoned McCutchan. "If they were enemy and they lived, it would make little difference to the war. But if they were friendly and we killed them, we could never bring them back to life."

Clay McCutchan told the controller he was leaving the area to return to base. He was not going to fire. "I was convinced I was going to get court-martialed because three times I disobeyed a direct order to fire," he told me. The commander met them as they landed at dawn. "You're either a hero or in a lot of trouble," he told McCutchan.

McCutchan spent a sleepless morning despite his fatigue. He had been up all night and in the air almost six hours. By noon the whole story came down from higher headquarters. Contact had been made with the troops surrounding the vehicles. McCutchan and his crew had been right: the troops were American Special Operations troops who had captured the enemy armored vehicles. They had been unsuccessful in contacting anyone by radio to identify themselves. McCutchan and the others on his crew were awarded medals for having the moral courage—the integrity—not to fire, even when ordered to do so.

Typical of an outstanding leader of integrity, McCutchan gave full credit to those he led. "My crew was very experienced. I was only an average pilot, but my copilot had 1,500 hours of combat in Vietnam. All of my officers and noncommissioned officers were very experienced and absolutely top-notch. It was my sole responsibility to make this decision, but I could not have made the decision I did if I did not trust them completely."[4]

McCutchan may or may not have been an average pilot. But the Air Force recognized that he was a far-above-average leader—a leader of integrity. Some years later Clay McCutchan became a major general.

Lose Your Integrity, Lose Your Career

The Center for Creative Leadership in Greensboro, North Carolina, conducted a groundbreaking study to identify traits or behaviors associated with eventual success or failure of top executives.[5] The researchers surveyed top managers and senior human resource executives. They gathered descriptions of twenty-one junior managers who had advanced into the ranks of middle or top management but had failed to perform successfully. These executives had been on the fast track, but they had all derailed. They were fired, opted for early retirement, or simply were never promoted again.

The researchers also obtained descriptions of twenty managers who had made it all the way to the top, and analyzed the two sets of descriptions to identify the similarities and differences between the failed and successful managers. Then they analyzed the extent to which various flaws were likely to derail a promising career. One major difference they uncovered was that those managers who were extremely successful were much more likely to have demonstrated strong integrity. Derailed managers were far more likely to have advanced their own careers at the expense of others. They were more likely to have betrayed a trust or broken a promise. An example given in the study was that of an executive who didn't implement a decision as promised. This caused conflicts and affected four levels of frustrated executives below him. These managers' failure didn't require major lapses in integrity of the sort that emerged at Enron or that contributed to the financial crisis of 2008 or that involved out-and-out fraud. Their slips were very basic. Yet they terminated many successful careers. Integrity is a fundamental law of Heroic Leadership in and out of the military.

No Cut-Off Date, No Limit Price

If you say something, make certain it is the exact truth. If you later realize you have misspoken, correct yourself. If you say you will do something, make certain you do it, no matter what.

Leonard Roberts became CEO of Arby's at a time when the business was doing very poorly. He turned the corporation around when sales had been falling 10 to 15 percent a year. He did this by promising service and support to Arby's franchisees with help and money. He delivered, and the franchisees supported him in turn. Sales soared.

Roberts was appointed to the board of directors. The first meeting he attended lasted fifteen minutes. The board was simply a rubber stamp for the owner. Eager for more profits, Arby's owner threatened to withdraw the help Roberts had given the franchisees. Moreover, bonuses earned by Roberts's staff would not be paid. Roberts immediately resigned from the board. The owner retaliated by firing Roberts for supporting the franchisees. But Roberts's sacrifice was not in vain. The integrity that he showed benefited the organization he left behind.[6]

Roberts went right into another situation calling for absolute integrity and Heroic Leadership. He was offered the position of chairman and CEO of Shoney's, a chain of two thousand restaurants headquartered in Nashville, Tennessee. The situation looked right, so Roberts accepted the offer. Only afterward did he learn that Shoney's was the subject of the largest racial discrimination lawsuit in history. Questioned by the *Wall Street Journal*, Roberts promised that the suit would be settled without long-term impact on the company. Unfortunately, this was more easily said than done. The case was not some kind of misunderstanding: the policy of the chairman was not to hire African-Americans. Moreover, he fired any restaurant manager who did! "The settlement of that suit was the thing I am most proud of in my life," says Len Roberts. "The former chairman agreed to pay up and settle. This saved the company. But I had to agree to resign after he did so. This was my second time out of work in almost as many years. My stand on integrity was getting kind of hard on my wife and kids. However, I knew it had to be done. There was no other way."

Roberts became the CEO of RadioShack after leaving Shoney's. A year after that he took on the additional job as CEO of the entire Tandy Corporation. This began a ten-year career of success with many honors. *Brandweek* magazine even named him Retail Marketer of the Year. Roberts says, "You cannot fake it—you must stand up for what is right regardless. You cannot maintain your integrity until it hurts your pocketbook or risks your job. You cannot maintain your integrity 90 percent and be a successful leader— it's got to be 100 percent."[7]

Pursue the "Harder Right"

As a young Air Force lieutenant in 1960 I was a new navigator on a B-52 crew. Among my responsibilities were two air-to-ground "cruise" missiles nicknamed "Hound Dogs." The missiles were also new and still had many problems that hadn't yet been solved; during simulated launch and impact they frequently didn't hit the target. We couldn't actually launch these highly sophisticated missiles. That would have cost tens of millions of dollars each in today's money. Instead, on practice runs I spent several hours programming the missiles and updating them with my navigational data so that their computers knew where they were within feet.

When we were about fifteen minutes from the target, I put the missile into a simulated launch mode. The pilots followed a special needle indicator on their consoles. If the needle turned right, the pilots turned the aircraft right; if the needle turned left, they turned the aircraft left. When they did this, the aircraft followed a course to the target according to information in the missile's inertial guidance system. A few seconds from the target the radar navigator turned on a tone signal. On the ground, a Ground Control Intercept (GCI) site tracked the aircraft on radar. At the point where the missile would have dived into its target, the missile automatically interrupted the tone signal. The course the missile would have taken to the ground once it started its final dive was based on predetermined factors. So when the tone signal stopped, the GCI site, plotting the aircraft's radar track and knowing the missile's ballistics, could easily calculate where the missile would have hit if it had actually been launched. The missile's accuracy generally depended on the accuracy of the information the navigator gave its computer during programming. These practice runs had a major impact on the crews' careers. Crews that got good scores, got promoted. Those that did not were held back.

My crewmates were all far more experienced than I was. My aircraft commander was a lieutenant colonel. All the other officers were senior. All were veterans of World War II or Korea; some, of both wars. We had never flown with missiles. One day, while we were on seven-day alert, the aircraft commander called the crew together. "We have missiles for the first time," he said. "I don't want to discuss it. We're going to cheat to make sure we get good scores. All I want to know is how we're going to do it."

I was shocked speechless. This went against everything I had been taught at West Point or in my limited time in the Air Force. The radar navigator spoke up. "That's easy. Don't follow the missile needle. I'll figure out an adjustment for the ballistics, and I'll 'bomb' the target using my bombsight. All you have to do is follow the bombsight's needle as we normally do. The GCI site will not know that we're actually bombing the target because we activate a tone in the same way as with the missiles."

We had three days of crew rest before getting together to plan the mission that would involve the twelve-hour flight with the missiles. The mission would include some regular bomb runs, some navigation and bomb runs at low level, an aerial refueling, a celestial navigation leg—and the simulated missile launch. The three days were absolute hell. I was new to the crew and the squadron but had heard rumors that this type of cheating was not unusual due to the extreme competition for promotion. Now I was being ordered to cheat with the very missiles with which I was entrusted. I talked it over with several other young lieutenants. They told me not to rock the boat. They said this sort of thing was not unusual and that everybody did it. If I didn't cheat occasionally, they said, it would be the end of my career.

I had worked long and hard for my career. I had worked long and hard to get to West Point, and with difficulty had managed to make it through my four years there. I had spent a year in navigation school and six months in bombardier school, had attended Air Force survival training, and had received more weeks of B-52 ground and air training. It had been six years altogether. How could I let it all slip away for refusing this one little lie that apparently nobody cared about anyway? Yet this lie was contrary to everything I had been taught and believed in about being an officer.

When my crew met to plan the mission, I asked to speak to my aircraft commander privately. As soon as we were alone, I told him, "If you want to cheat on these missiles, that's up to you. But get yourself a new navigator, because I'm not going to do it." He was furious and berated me for quite a long time. Then he left the room, slamming the door. I was plenty scared, and I thought it was the end of my career.

An hour or so later he was still angry when he said he wanted to see me alone. Once we were alone, he said, "Okay. We'll do it your way. And this won't affect your performance report. But those missiles better be reliable." I told him that I would do everything possible to make them so, but I wouldn't cheat. Later I heard that this aircraft commander had told someone, "I don't know whether Bill's a good navigator or not, but I trust him. He's honest, and he's got guts."

The missiles were reliable. To this day I don't know if I was skilled or lucky, or whether the two lieutenant colonels had figured out a way to fool their inexperienced young navigator. But here's something I did know. I knew how far I would go for what I believed to be right. And the answer: all the way. I believe this knowledge has helped me immensely over the years, and I believe that I owe whatever success I have achieved in part to this decision to do the "harder right." In fact that decision still affects my thinking today. Had it ended my career then and there, it still would have been worth this priceless piece of knowledge about myself.

You are in the same position. If you haven't met this test yet, you will. If you already have and passed it, congratulations; you're on the right path. If you failed, don't make the same mistake twice. You don't have to. The past does not equal the future. And it's never too late.

Guard Your Principles

As I've said, integrity doesn't only mean being honest and talking straight. It means being trustworthy and principled.

I met George Brown before he retired from his civilian career. He stood tall and straight, and was respected by all who knew him. After his military service he had gone back to school under the G.I. Bill. Eventually, he got his doctorate and became a university professor. As I was getting into the "professor business," George was getting ready to retire. In the university, his leadership skills and integrity were practiced in one of the most trying environments outside of combat: the college classroom. And George excelled.

By the time he became professor emeritus, he had won numerous awards for teaching. He was equally popular with students, faculty, and administrators.

When I was just starting out as a professor, George took his fellow (former) "warrior" under his wing. He told me the above story as well as the one that I am about to tell you.

During George's first year at the university, it was rumored that some professors were cutting their night school classes and letting students leave early. Evening classes started at 6:00 P.M. and continued until 10:00 P.M. with a twenty-minute break at the midway point. These professors were dismissing their classes as much as an hour early. Apparently, the chancellor's office had got wind of what was going on from student complaints. The chancellor told the deans that he would send someone around to monitor the classes unannounced. Professors not teaching their full class periods would be disciplined. Those professors, like George, who were not yet tenured would be dismissed for the same cause.

George's dean sent warnings to all professors teaching night classes to teach their full class periods. George had been following the rules and wasn't worried. However, only days after the chancellor's announcement and the dean's warning, George ran into a problem.

In one of his night classes he had invited guest speakers to lecture at two sessions. Each speaker would lecture for an hour, followed by a half hour answering questions. There would be a short break, and George would then lecture for the final two hours and ten minutes. The first session had worked out fine. But George was young and still inexperienced. He was not prepared for an unexpected turn of events.

Unfortunately, that was exactly what happened: George's guest speaker did not show up. Several years later this would have been no problem. By that time George would have enough material and be experienced enough to simply cover a few hours of the following week's lesson. However, as a new professor George was only slightly ahead of the students. He had two hours and ten minutes of lecture to present that night, perhaps a few minutes more. But that was it.

The Man in White

Normally, George would have dismissed the class early, felt a little stupid, learned his own lesson from what had happened, and moved on. However, George remembered the dean's warning about monitors from the chancellor's office. And sure enough, on this one night when his speaker didn't show, a stranger showed up dressed in an all-white suit with a black tie. George knew this man had to be the monitor from the chancellor's office.

As George began his two-hour lecture, he reviewed his options. He could drag his lecture out and think up some time-wasting activities. With a little luck and by dragging the break out a little longer, he could probably stretch things to 10:00 P.M. The alternative didn't look so good. Even if he took a twenty-minute break in the middle of his two-hour-and-ten-minute lecture, he would still be releasing his students more than an hour early.

George had had a hard time finding his job. There hadn't been many professorial openings the year he completed his graduate degree. And now George feared that he stood an excellent chance of losing his job. Not a terrific prospect, especially since he and his wife had a two-year-old baby girl to feed. They surely weren't going to be able to manage on his wife's salary as a secretary.

As George continued to lecture, he wrestled with himself. He knew that the right thing to do did not include wasting forty students' time because of his own inexperience and lack of preparation. At the halfway point he announced a twenty-minute break. "I really hadn't admitted to myself that I was going to let them go early, what with 'the man in white' there and everything," he told me. "But I guess in my heart of hearts, I knew. Any leader, in the classroom or out, must do the right thing or he will lose his self-respect."

At the end of his lecture George told the class what had happened and took full responsibility. He announced that they would be excused more than an hour early, and he recommended that they use the time to study. The students applauded. George's heart sank: *The man in white just wrote something down in a book*, he noticed to himself.

That night he told his wife. "Well, I screwed up, and I may get fired." She told him not to worry. She said it would all work out.

The next day one of his female students came to his office. "I hope you didn't mind," she said. "I enjoy your lectures so much that I invited my fiancé to attend last night. I didn't have an opportunity to introduce him to you, but he was the one in the white suit and black tie. He's a host at a restaurant and came right from work."

"I never felt so relieved and so foolish all at the same time," George related. "I was relieved that I wouldn't be losing my job, but I think I was even more relieved when I realized how close I had come to wasting more than forty student-hours simply because one of my students brought her fiancé to class!"

In contrast, many corporate executives don't blink an eye at permanently discharging thousands of loyal employees. They will state that integrity is important, and if asked they would probably say that the firings "go against their principles" but that they had "no choice." They offer little or nothing to most of their employees to ease the pain of dismissal. Yet many of these employees have worked for the organization their entire careers. Moreover, in many of these corporations CEOs take big bonuses and salary increases even as they fire employees.

Even when layoffs are necessary for the survival of a company— as in times of great economic challenge—two cautionary notes can be held up for company executives who want to maintain absolute integrity. First, leadership should share the pain through its own salary cuts. Second, everything possible should be done to ease the pain of those who must be terminated.

Summary

Maintaining absolute integrity is the bottom-line rule for leaders who expect subordinates to follow under any and all conditions—to hell and back, that is. You can develop your integrity if you will

- Keep your word.
- Choose the harder right over the easier wrong.
- Guard your principles.

CHAPTER 2

• •

Know Your Stuff

• •

During World War II, the U.S. Army conducted a study to find out what soldiers thought about their leaders. The researchers, including professors from Harvard, Princeton, and the University of Chicago, surveyed tens of thousands of soldiers. They asked, "What are the most important factors associated with good leadership?" The most frequent answer these researchers received was "that the leader know his stuff."[1]

My West Point classmate Lieutenant Colonel Bill Schwartz fought and led in Vietnam in two combat tours as an infantry officer.[2] Afterward he became director of international marketing for Litton Applied Technology in San Jose, California. When I interviewed him for an earlier book on leadership, he said, "I am most proud of the fact that no one lost his life under my command because I made a mistake. Job competence is crucial because leaders lacking it waste lives and frequently still fail to accomplish the mission."

• • • •

During World War I, Corporal Alvin C. York was a soldier in Company G, 328th Regiment, 82nd Division of the U.S. Army.

No one noticed anything particularly unusual about him when he was drafted—that is, until he filed to avoid military service as a conscientious objector. But his new company commander convinced him to stay on. York went overseas to France with his unit.

There was one other item of interest in York's background. It made him very attractive as a combat infantryman. It may also help explain why his company commander tried so hard to keep him. York was an expert shot. He had been a champion marksman in his home state of Tennessee before the war. As a rifleman he really knew his stuff. His company commander felt York's knowledge and skill in marksmanship would be very handy to have on the battlefield. As it turned out, this became more important in France than anyone could have imagined.

By 1918 York was a corporal. On October 18 he was sent on a patrol in the Argonne Forest with sixteen other men under the command of a sergeant. The patrol managed to surprise a German headquarters and took several prisoners. As the patrol moved on, they stumbled on a hidden nest of enemy machine guns and were themselves surprised. The machine guns opened fire with deadly effectiveness. Only York and seven privates survived the first volley. Corporal York was suddenly thrust into the role of leader in a very perilous situation.

The seven privates wanted to surrender. York asked them to wait. He told them to keep under cover and guard their prisoners. Then he began to look for a position from which to fire at the Germans. You can imagine what must have gone through the minds of those young privates. York had only one thing going for him: they knew that he was an expert marksman. He knew his stuff.

Corporal York found a good spot from which to shoot. He could see the enemy clearly, but they could not see him. He fired several shots and then moved to a new position. He repeated the process. By the time a machine gun would begin to fire at him, York had already moved. Meanwhile, he was able to get a couple of shots off at the Germans manning the guns; he rarely missed. The enemy was helpless against his relentless sniping, as man after man fell to his marksmanship. They must have thought they were facing a large number of Americans.

The Germans then sent out a squad of eight armed infantrymen. York had a clear view of them as they approached. He fired, working the rifle's bolt as rapidly as he could. Before they could fire a single shot, he had dropped all eight. York moved again to another position, where he resumed shooting at the machine-gun crews.

As more soldiers fell to York's bullets, the German commander, it seems, could do nothing. Little did he know that the deadly fire came from a single man. Thinking he must be surrounded by a larger force, he surrendered his command. With only the seven privates helping, York captured another 132 prisoners, including three officers.

The Supreme Allied Commander, the French Marshal Ferdinand Foch, had been at war for four years. He was aware of the daily actions of millions of men in battle. He saw hundreds of situations where courageous leaders had performed heroic deeds. Foch called York's feat the greatest individual action of the war. General Pershing, the overall American commander, immediately promoted York to sergeant and recommended him for the Congressional Medal of Honor. This is America's highest decoration for valor, and Sergeant York received it shortly thereafter.

Now look at the facts of York's exploit again from a leadership perspective. York was a very brave man and a highly skilled marksman. However, had he not been able to persuade his men not to surrender, it is unlikely that he would have been able to accomplish anything. Unguarded, their former prisoners would soon have informed the German commander that only one man opposed his battalion. Would the commander have surrendered to York then? Surely he and his men would have attacked in overwhelming numbers.

York's privates obeyed his order not to surrender even though they faced overwhelming odds, but this was only because they knew that York was such an extraordinary marksman. York had been their leader for only a few moments, but they knew that in this respect their leader knew his stuff. Between the wars, York was commissioned in the Tennessee National Guard, and he served during World War II as a colonel.

Knowing Your Stuff, Whatever You Do

You'd think that "knowing your stuff" would be an obvious requirement in either military or civilian life. Yet it is unfortunately true that some leaders don't know their stuff to the extent they should. Their emphasis is less on becoming an expert and learning their trade than on getting ahead. This leads to a focus on office politics rather than professional expertise.

Moreover, a number of management books fall into this same trap in advising readers. They fail to emphasize that people become real leaders when those who would follow them recognize that their leaders know *what* to do after getting ahead, not because they know *how* to get ahead. People don't follow leaders because they are good at office politics; they follow them because they are good at what they do. There is no substitute for a leader investing enough time into becoming an expert. As *Fortune* once proclaimed, "Forget about fighting over titles and turf—it's what you know (and how you use it) that really counts."[3]

Bill Gates's Advantage

Bill Gates was the chairman of Microsoft Corporation, which he founded and built himself. His personal fortune has been estimated at $58 billion (that's billion with a *b*). Amazingly, he achieved much of his success while he was still in his twenties. He became a billionaire when he was only thirty-one. Was he just there at the right time and right place? Was Gates just lucky? Did people of means and ability lend him money, acknowledge him as a leader, and help him build his giant corporation because of his academic credentials? Because of his Hollywood-handsome looks? His influential parents? Hardly. Bill Gates went to Harvard, but he dropped out after only two years. He wears glasses. Some say he looks almost nerdish. His father was an attorney, and his mother, a schoolteacher.

If you look at Gates's career, you can see that he took the time to learn his stuff. His secret was not office politics but the expert power he acquired. Gates started learning how to program computers when he was thirteen. By the time he entered high school, he knew enough to lead a group of computer programmers who were computerizing his school's payroll system. While still a teenager, he started a company that sold traffic-counting systems to local governments. By the time he entered Harvard, he was already an acknowledged computer expert. He spent his freshman year preparing the language for the world's first microcomputer. His second year was more of the same. Then he decided to drop out so he could work full time at developing computer software. Not long after that he founded the Microsoft Corporation.

Others followed Gates because in this new field of computer programming Gates was top gun. They didn't care how young he was. They didn't care that he wasn't 6'5", or who his parents were, or were not, or whether he had a college degree. Gates simply knew his stuff. Today newspapers and magazines frequently carry news of Gates's latest exploits. He makes news today, not because of his wealth but because he is successful; and people still follow him because he still knows his stuff. General Sir John Hackett, an experienced battlefield commander and principal of Kings College (London), wrote in his international best-seller *The Third World War* that "the leader, besides being a competent manager, must be known to possess a high degree of competence in some specific skill or skills closely relevant to the discharge of the organization's primary task."[4]

Study Overcomes Odds

Some say we cannot learn much from the young, but that sim-
ply isn't so. A nineteen-year-old American wanted to join the Air
Corps and become a pilot back in 1940. This was shortly before the
United States entered World War II. Unfortunately, Chesley "Pete"
Peterson could not pass the Army's eye exam. One day he learned
that the British were looking for volunteers for the Royal Air
Force. England was already in the war and was short of pilots. The
RAF decided to form a squadron made up entirely of Americans.
Because the British needed pilots badly, the vision standards for
pilots weren't as high as in the United States. Peterson took the
flight physical for the RAF and passed. They sent him to Canada
for pilot training. Before long he was a fighter pilot in one of the
two American Eagle Squadrons flying Spitfires against the best
pilots in the German Luftwaffe. What happened next shows the
importance of both technical expertise and leadership expertise.

Peterson's squadron was in combat above England almost
every day. Needless to say, there was considerable danger. Losses
were high. Many pilots lived pretty wild lives on the ground, and
Peterson could party with the best of them. But during periods
of combat operations he didn't waste his time partying. Instead,
he took the time to become an expert fighter pilot. Peterson read
everything he could find about air combat, and he sought out other
pilots, talking with them at great length. Every night he went
through a lengthy ritual. Before going to sleep, he went over every
minute of the fights he had engaged in with the enemy during the
day. He reviewed what had gone right and what had gone wrong.
He thought about what he had done that worked and what had
not worked. He analyzed his mistakes and considered how he could
avoid them in the future. He planned what he would do differently
the next day.

Before long, Peterson shot down his first enemy aircraft. And
then another. And after that, another. It wasn't long before he

had shot down five enemy aircraft. This gave him the designation "ace." Peterson was now an expert fighter pilot. Would it surprise you to learn that though he was one of the youngest pilots in his squadron, they chose Peterson when they needed a new squadron commander?

Squadron Leader Peterson continued to follow his plan in a search for further excellence. Now he worked at becoming an expert squadron commander. He followed the same routine, so he learned fast. When the RAF needed a new wing commander, again they selected Pete Peterson. Meanwhile, he stuck with his plan. When they needed a group commander—well, you can guess the rest.

By 1943 the United States was very much in the war. Now it was the Americans who needed experienced pilots. With the concurrence of the RAF they transferred Peterson's entire unit to the U.S. Army Air Force, which gave Peterson the equivalent rank to the one he had held in the RAF. Peterson thus became a colonel in the U.S. Army Air Force at the age of twenty-three. He was the youngest colonel in that service.

Pete Peterson stayed with the U.S. Air Force after World War II. Twenty years later he was promoted to general, still only in his early forties. I'm certain that much of Peterson's success was that he always took the time to learn his stuff. I don't know whether Peterson knew anything about office politics, but I rather think he did not.

Learn from Every Experience

Every experience as a leader teaches something—the failures perhaps more than the successes. In fact you may be able to make the argument that the more failures you have and the bigger they are, the greater your potential for success. So long as you learn from your experiences.

George Washington was made commander in chief of the American forces, having no top-level command experience, because there simply was no one else for the job who had that kind of experience either. Previously, he had been a major in the British Army. Washington blundered badly at first, so much so that his mistakes could have ended the American Revolution less than two months after the Declaration of Independence.

What did he do wrong? First, he deferred to the Continental Congress's demand in 1776 that he defend New York, even though he knew that to do so would threaten the very existence of his army—and American independence. Once having made this decision, he split his army, putting one third under the able Major General Nathanael Greene on Long Island and retaining the remainder under his personal command on Manhattan to prevent the British from attacking up the Hudson. Greene's selection was a good choice, but splitting his army was dangerous. The two forces were not mutually supporting, and the British could have concentrated first against one and then the other, easily defeating both.

When General Greene fell ill, Washington blundered again. He chose Major General Israel Putnam as Greene's replacement. Unfortunately, General Putnam needed a very short leash. Washington should have kept him on one until he better knew his capabilities. Instead, he trusted Putnam in this critical assignment and supervised him little, even though Putnam was mostly an unknown quantity. But that wasn't all. Washington didn't make the command relationship between himself and Putnam clear. Putnam didn't know whether he had an independent command and could do as he saw fit, or whether he should function under Washington's immediate direction.

Meanwhile, Washington's opponent, the British general Howe, shifted the bulk of his forces to Long Island. He discovered that Putnam had made a basic error. The American left flank was not secured along the Brooklyn Heights. In fact it was "in the air." Howe easily brought ten thousand men around Putnam's left flank and encircled his army. Putnam's defense collapsed. Washington then compounded his earlier errors. He took reinforcements to Long Island, which only had the effect of moving additional troops into the trap. The river couldn't be crossed at this point and so couldn't be supported or reinforced easily. Washington's army was in the perfect position to be totally destroyed. He was saved only because Howe failed to attack—a decision so bizarre that historians can only speculate that perhaps the British commander hoped the Americans would rejoin the mother country with minimum bloodshed. In plain fact, the Americans came very close to losing the war. On the night of August 29–30, Washington wisely evacuated his troops and withdrew.

Eventually, Washington was pushed out of New York City proper, and he reestablished a defensive position near White Plains. Here again he split his army, placing half under the command of the ambitious and incompetent Major General Charles Lee. The only thing that saved the loss of Lee's entire command was that Lee himself managed to get himself captured by the British, thus removing top-level incompetence from the American ranks. On December 26, Washington won a small but important victory at Trenton, New Jersey, by crossing the Delaware River. (You've probably seen the famous painting entitled *Washington Crossing the Delaware*; this is the event the painting commemorates.) However, soon after his victory Washington realized that he had erred again. He had left his right flank unprotected, just as Putnam had done. It was exposed to British attack. If that flank were turned, he would have no place to go but back toward the sea.

With all these mistakes, Washington was learning his trade. Washington learned from every experience. He didn't dwell on his errors. He analyzed the situation, drew conclusions, and noted what he had done wrong and right. He planned how he would react in the future.

Washington slipped around the British secretly by using icy back roads. He made a forced march to Princeton, where he had numerical superiority over the enemy. Through this action, he surprised, attacked, and defeated three British regiments. These were part of another British command under General Cornwallis, which was much larger than the American's. Washington couldn't take General Cornwallis's army on head to head; he lacked the strength. But astride Cornwallis's line of communications he forced the British to evacuate all of central and western New Jersey lest their forces be cut off without supplies and forced to surrender. Frederick the Great called this ten-day campaign, beginning with the crossing of the Delaware, "one of the most brilliant in military history"—and that despite the mistakes.[5]

Failure Can Lead to Success

Self-made millionaire Wayne Allyn Root actually organized the idea into a formalized structure and wrote a book about it, *The Joy of Failure*. Root himself said that after getting rejected by law school he lost a political election and then drove his real estate business into the ground. "I failed at twelve careers and businesses," he says.[6] He learned from every failure, however.

John Macy failed—and learned—in seven attempts at department stores before he founded the business that caught on and that yet bears his name, 150 years later and in 810 stores employing 182,000 (in the United States alone). It is said that Thomas Edison failed at more than a thousand attempts to invent the light bulb. It seemed that every material he tried for the filament burned up. While many of us would call each attempt another failure, Edison had it right. Declared America's most versatile inventor, "I have not failed. I have learned yet another material that will not work as a filament."

"Colonel" Harland Sanders received his first social security check and decided it wasn't enough to live on. He then went on the road and spent two years trying to sell owners of fast-food restaurants on the idea of using his recipe for Kentucky fried chicken. He didn't ask for any money up front, only that the owner try his recipe and, if successful, give him a few pennies from each sale. Every single owner he approached turned him down. But Sanders learned from each rejection. He improved his presentation. He did more research. He learned to handle every possible objection. Finally, after two years he got a single acceptance. And then another, and another after that. Like all practitioners of Heroic Leadership, Sanders never stopped learning.

Norm Brodsky, founder and still president of CitiStorage, an archive-retrieval business in Brooklyn, and past *Inc.* 500 business owner, once wrote, "You will never stop making mistakes. We hope that the new ones won't be the same as the old ones, but I promise you they'll be just as painful. . . . But, as upset as you may get, it's important to bear in mind that failure is still the best teacher. You'll do fine as long as you're open to the lessons it's trying to teach you."[7]

Summary

If you want to be a Heroic Leader, don't waste your time learning how to defend your turf or be perceived as a fast burner. Instead,

- Know your people.
- Become an expert.
- Learn from every experience.

CHAPTER 3

• •

Declare Your Expectations

• •

A leader's expectations can be seen as falling into two categories. The first tends to be tactical and of shorter term. These expectations have to do with immediate tasks and short-term and intermediate goals and objectives. The second has to do with the leader's vision for the organization. The word *vision* calls up an image of the leader seeing a picture of the organization in the future—what it will become and how it will look. Both sets of expectations are important. If the leader's vision of the organization is fuzzy and vague, the organization will probably be unsuccessful in the long term no matter how well the shorter-term tasks, goals, and objectives are formulated and executed. This is because these tactical expectations may be taking the firm to a less than optimum future. On the other hand, a clear, sharp, well-thought-out, and worthwhile vision may never be reached should the shorter-term class of expectations be drawn up poorly or be well-drawn but neglected.

• • • •

During the Vietnam War, Ted Crichton was given command of a squadron flying four-engine C-130 transports out of Danang, Vietnam, and later Ubon, Thailand. Ted's squadron had an unusual and difficult mission, and Ted's job was to accomplish that mission with an aircraft intended for combat support, not combat flying. The lumbering C-130 transport was to be used as a night controller of fighters attacking heavily defended targets over North Vietnam and Laos.

Crichton soon learned that his huge C-130s had to make rapid high-g maneuvers called "jinking" to avoid the fire of anti-aircraft guns. But the C-130 was built as a transport aircraft and was not designed to take the high stress loads from jinking. Moreover, to accomplish the mission the C-130 had to open its giant cargo doors in the air. The limiting speed for safety with the doors open was 150 knots. Above this speed the additional stress could cause the structural integrity of the aircraft to fail. While 150 knots (172.5 miles per hour) was the safety limit with open doors, the C-130 needed to fly at up to 250 knots or 287.5 miles an hour for effective jinking. To jink at a slower speed would not be as effective and could cause the aircraft to stall. With the addition of a flare dispenser (to hold the flares used to illuminate targets on the ground) the lower door could be locked, but not the upper one. Although there was little danger of a wing or control surface failing, higher stress created loads on the airplane that could cause the upper door to open and damage the structure holding the tail surfaces in place. This could induce additional problems in flying the aircraft, even causing it to crash.

Ted informed higher headquarters of the problem. They contacted the Lockheed Aircraft Company, which built the aircraft. Meanwhile, Ted and his squadron had to jink their aircraft every night despite the danger of structural damage to the airplane. Ted credits the solution to this problem to the third universal law of Heroic Leadership: Declare your expectations. He didn't mandate a solution, because he had none to offer. Instead, every chance he got, he declared his expectation that someone in the squadron would solve the problem. Eventually, someone in the crew did exactly that. Every time the C-130 jinked, the crew made certain that maximum hydraulic pressure was exerted on the door to hold it closed; they did this by working a hand pump that was designed to restore hydraulic pressure if it was ever lost in an emergency. This additional hydraulic pressure on the door in effect raised the stress limit by increasing the force holding the door closed. This was not a solution that higher headquarters liked. Lockheed wouldn't certify Crichton's solution, and it wasn't certified by the Air Force either. But when there was nothing else available, it worked.

After retiring from the Air Force as a brigadier general, Ted became president of American Nucleonics Corporation. Ted credits his success there partly to the same universal law of leadership. "Constant discussion with your people of your expectations . . . what you are trying to do and how you are doing . . . is always the key," he says.[1]

Vision

What is vision, anyway? It's an all-encompassing picture of the way you want your organization to look in the future. Without a vision, your organization is as helpless as a leaderless brood of caterpillars. Without a vision, you'll never get "there"—and neither will your organization. Just like Bloody Mary's song in *South Pacific*, "If you don't have a dream . . . if you don't have a dream, how you gonna make a dream come true?"

In his most famous speech, Dr. Martin Luther King Jr. told us, "I have a dream." King went on to describe a very different kind of America than existed at that time—one in which people weren't judged by the color of their skin but by the content of their character. Dr. King's vision changed America forever.

Sam Walton built a spectacular retail chain from a vision of providing quality goods to people in geographical areas that major retailers were not serving. He felt so strongly about his vision that he risked his personal future and well-being, leaving a well-paid executive position at J.C. Penney to implement it. Wal-Mart was the fruit of his powerful vision.

Vision and Success

All successful organizations, whether small businesses, Fortune 500 companies, athletic teams, combat units, or even countries must be built on a clear and compelling vision. Vision provides direction for everyone. It guides all action and tells everyone exactly where the organization is going. With sufficient commitment to their leader's vision, members of the organization willingly work toward it; almost miraculously, such an organization usually attains that vision, sometimes in every single detail.

Barack Obama electrified the world by becoming, against all odds, the first African-American president of the United States. A few years earlier he had been mostly unknown. He had been in the U.S. Senate less than two years. His primary opponent in his own party was Senator Hillary Clinton. Not only did Clinton have eight years in the Senate, but she was extremely well known as former president Bill Clinton's wife. She had many accomplishments to her credit and many political contacts. If Obama somehow succeeded in gaining the nomination of his party over Clinton, he would be running against a popular war hero, another senator. Senator John McCain had many more years of experience in the Senate and a long list of accomplishments. Yet Barack Obama won. How was this possible?

Of course there were many reasons for Obama's victory, including his intelligence, charisma, and likability, and the fact that he ran a nearly flawless campaign. Chuck Todd, who had been the NBC News political director and named NBC White House correspondent after the election, wrote a book analyzing that 2008 presidential campaign entitled *How Barack Obama Won* (Vintage, 2009). One of the interesting facts he uncovered was mentioned in a *Today Show* interview with Matt Lauer: of the three leading candidates, Obama was the only one to state his expectations for the country; and of the three, he was the only one, in an announcement speech, to declare both his candidacy *and* his vision.[2]

I know that may sound oversimplified, but the truth is, some leaders just don't know what they want for their organizations' futures. They may not know what they want at all, beyond their organizations to be "successful." But until the leader defines exactly what success means, both personally and for the organization, there is no hope. To be a successful leader, you must take the time to get your expectations very clear in your mind.

Lieutenant General Jack V. Mackmull served in combat in Vietnam and has had the distinction of having commanded infantry, aviation, paratrooper, and special warfare units. Reflecting on his experiences, he notes, "You've got to begin by analyzing the mission requirements to determine what tasks need to be accomplished."[3] You can't get "there" until you know where "there" is.

Mighty Charles Atlas

Whenever I think of compelling expectations, I cannot help but think of Charles Atlas, of whom you may have heard, and Charles Roman, of whom you probably have not. Charles Atlas was a poor Italian boy who immigrated to the United States around the turn of the last century. His real name was Angelo Siciliano. As a boy Angelo was painfully weak—a ninety-eight-pound weakling, in fact. After a rough beating by a bully, he cried himself to sleep but swore an oath that no man on earth would ever hurt him again. Health clubs didn't exist at that time, and he had no money to buy weights, so he had to develop a unique method of bodybuilding. He began to experiment. In twelve months he doubled his body weight. He entered bodybuilding contests and won. Then he became a well-known artist's model. Among the famous sculptures for which he served as a model are those depicting Alexander Hamilton, in front of the U.S. Treasury Building

in Washington, D.C.; George Washington, in New York City's
Washington Square; and the "Dawn of Glory" in Brooklyn's Prospect
Park. Using his prize money from the contests and his modeling,
Atlas developed a bodybuilding correspondence course and began to
sell it through the mail. However, he couldn't get enough customers
with his advertisements, and he began to lose money. Married, with
two children, no income, and a floundering business, Atlas was in
serious trouble. Enter Charles Roman.

Charles Roman worked at the Benjamin Landsman Advertising Agency of New York. In desperation, Atlas asked the Landsman
agency for help. Roman was a recent graduate of New York
University. As the most recent hire, he was given the account with
the worst potential: Charles Atlas. Roman read over Atlas's course
materials and realized that the ads simply didn't make Atlas's
expectations for his prospects compelling. Roman came up with
new ways of doing this. Four months after their meeting, Atlas
and Roman became partners. "The Insult That Made a Man Out
of Mac," one headline trumpeted. And Roman invited respon-
dents to check the kind of body they wanted: "Broader Chest
and Shoulders," "Ironhard Stomach Muscles," "Tireless Legs,"
"Slimmer Waist and Legs," "More Energy and Stamina"; the list
went on and on. From a few hundred courses sold, the number
climbed to three thousand in the first year of business together.
Soon it reached ten thousand. In 1971, the year before Atlas died,
they sold more than twenty-three thousand courses worldwide.[4]
The course is still selling today.

Here's the point: Charles Atlas declared his expectations for
his potential customers, but until Roman came on the scene, he
did not do so in a sufficiently compelling fashion. Once Roman
made the expectations compelling, prospects were influenced
to buy—and buy in a big way. Leaders declaring their expectations in order to influence those who follow them are much
like retailers attempting to influence prospects to buy. Successful
leaders do so by first making certain that their expectations are

formulated in a compelling fashion. Part of Obama's vision and expectation was change, but his compelling expectation was, "Yes, we can!"

Ask Why

To be compelling, expectations have to bring strong benefits to the organization once they are achieved. What benefits will result once you have turned your expectations into reality? Will your customers be better off? How? Will the members of your organization be happier or achieve more in their careers? Will society benefit? Will your organization be acclaimed number one in its field? Think through in detail the benefits of your expectations. Ask yourself, "Why these specific expectations?"

R. J. "Zap" Zlatoper is a modern admiral who asked, "Why?" and made his expectations compelling in a very dramatic fashion. Admiral Zlatoper flew combat missions off a carrier during the Vietnam War, and he commanded major naval combat units during Operation Desert Storm. As a four-star admiral, "Zap" Zlatoper commanded the entire Pacific Fleet. Then he retired and became CEO of Sanchez Computer Associates in Malvern, Pennsylvania. A $19 million business, Sanchez offers integrated software solutions and services for financial institutions worldwide.

Says Admiral Zlatoper, "Sanchez was and is a great company with terrific people. But they really didn't understand what it really meant to work together. So, I took my top executives out to the USS *Enterprise* aircraft carrier to watch the extraordinary coordination and teamwork necessary to launch and recover naval warplanes at sea. It requires split-second timing and the precise interaction of hundreds of people. One screw-up or prima donna can spell disaster, so you can't have any. They saw what I wanted of them, and they did it. I can't help but think this new orientation has contributed to our hypergrowth, and our stock going from $5 to $32 a share."[5] Zlatoper had asked why being able to work together was of such potential benefit to the team. He didn't need to say much more. On the deck of the *Enterprise* that day, the reason was compelling. It went further. During Zlatoper's tenure as CEO (from 1997 to 2000), Sanchez Computer Associates grew to a $1 billion corporation.[6]

You will need to know and understand the likely benefits of fulfilling your expectations if you are to communicate your vision to others. You need to have these benefits fixed in your own mind and soul as you progress toward achieving your goals. Without knowing why, you will not be able to convince yourself or others that the sacrifices are worthwhile once the going gets tough—as it always will. Without knowing why, you will abandon your vision before it can be attained. Without knowing why, your expectations cannot be compelling. In contrast, by knowing the specific benefits that will accrue when you complete your task or achieve your goal, objective, or vision, you will gain great leverage for yourself and your organization, leverage which will help you reach your version of success.

Plan and Implement

There is a very old saying that those who fail to plan, plan to fail. Planning is a process of thinking things through. You have established precisely where you want to go and why you must get there. Now you must establish exactly how you are going to do this. Start by scanning your environment. Combat leaders have been doing this for thousands of years. Those that fight on the ground call it reconoitering. They do it and then come up with something they call the *estimate of the situation*. They look at alternative courses of action to reach their objective, and then decide on the best one. You must do the same. Major General Don H. Payne, who saw combat in the Air Force in both Korea and Vietnam, says, "Plan as meticulously as the situation allows. Generally, the more time and resources available for detailed planning, the more likely is success and reduced losses."[7] Sometimes reaching your final objective requires breaking the goal up into smaller tasks. You can eat an elephant, but only if you eat it one bite at a time. So you may need to break your larger goal down into smaller, doable bites.

Although you can do it in your head, many leaders find it useful to write their plans down with firm dates for reaching each expectation. I like that. It's a way of getting even greater leverage for yourself and your organization to attain your goals.

Once you have your plan, you can start working it. When you start implementing a plan, you will see that not everything will work out exactly as you originally thought. That's okay. The important thing is to start it, stay with it, and adjust your plan as you proceed. Sure, you are going to run into obstacles. That's normal. The simple fact that your organization is progressing toward a goal will give it the momentum to continue.

Promote Your Expectations

Promoting your expectations means putting forward what you want your organization to do, what its values are, where you want your organization to go, and what you want your organization to be. Think about your expectations, use them as a basis of discussion, talk about them and write about them every chance you get. Tie them in to everything you do. Every time someone takes an action which moves you toward a hoped-for outcome of your expectations, let people know. Give them a pat on the back. As Mark Victor Hansen, co-originator of the *Chicken Soup* book series, once suggested, don't just check off your list of expectations as they are achieved; declare a victory. Heroic Leaders promote their expectations at every opportunity. Heroic Leaders know they must dramatize their expectations as they promote them. Many combat leaders condense their expectations into brief messages that have a dramatic impact and get repeated again and again. MacArthur promised, "I shall return." Commodore Dewey declared, "Damn the torpedoes, full speed ahead." Captain John Paul Jones won a battle by telling everyone, "I have not yet begun to fight." During Operation Desert Storm, a newsman asked

General Colin Powell the strategy for defeating Saddam Hussein's army. Powell answered, "First we are going to cut it off, and then we are going to kill it." General Powell's answer reached every soldier in every language of the allied forces fighting in the war.

Listen to Feedback

Robert Townsend, who served in the U.S. Navy during World War II, was president of Avis Rent a Car during its period of greatest growth. It was he who sponsored the "We Try Harder" theme, which is still used today. Townsend once reported that one of his vice presidents who disagreed with a proposed action sent him a note that began, "If you insist, it will be my duty to make it so. However, I must respectfully tell you that you are full of shit again." Townsend never punished subordinates for speaking their mind. He felt it was all part of the "We Try Harder" philosophy. In fact, the "We Try Harder" advertising campaign only started when Townsend found that he could scrape together a million dollars to spend on advertising but that the competition was spending five times that. Townsend's idea was to find something really outstanding about Avis that could be promoted. After interviewing a dozen advertising agencies, he hired Doyle Dane Bernbach. Bill Bernbach studied the company for three months. At the end of this period, he told Townsend that there wasn't anything really outstanding about the company, but that Avis did try harder than others, and since Avis wasn't close to being number one, he thought he could craft a campaign based on these two facts. Townsend listened to this feedback and scrapped the original strategy he proposed. Avis' internal sales growth rate increased 10 to 35 percent. When Robert Townsend became president of Avis, it had been in the red for thirteen years. He turned Avis around in one year.

Listening to feedback and adjusting strategy as needed helps to clarify your expectations. It is part of the third universal law of Heroic Leadership.

Summary

You can't get "there" until you know where or what it is. In Heroic Leadership "there" is your set of expectations for your organization. To help the entire organization get there,

- Clarify your expectations.
- Make your expectations compelling.
- Develop a plan and implement it.
- Promote—and dramatize—your expectations.
- Listen to feedback and adjust your strategy as needed.

CHAPTER 4

. . . .

Show Uncommon Commitment

. . . .

You don't have to read much military history to see that successful leaders in battle are extraordinarily committed to their jobs. This goes far beyond simple determination to succeed. The successful battle leader—the Heroic Leader—breathes, sleeps, and eats the mission. That does not mean that the leader doesn't relax after the project, task, or mission is completed; the leader need not be a workaholic. As a matter of fact, Heroic Leaders do have time for friends, family, and recreation when not completing an important task. But their extraordinary commitment seems to attract others to work and fight to achieve the organization's goal. As retired Army Brigadier General Edward Markham, director of Management Information Systems in Lubbock, Texas, explains, "A leader must take a bulldog approach to accomplish the mission."[1] When the leader does this, others do the same.

. . . .

On June 25, 1950, Communist North Korea suddenly invaded South Korea with the aim of unifying the country under its rule.

47

The Air Force sent First Lieutenant Pat Patterson to the Eighth Fighter-Bomber Group in Korea flying the F-80 "Shooting Star," America's first operational jet fighter.

Patterson learned something about the power of uncommon commitment on his one hundredth mission. Patterson was group leader. "We were to hit the bridges on the Yalu connecting China with North Korea. It was the farthest north in Korea I had ever been." Patterson would be leading the entire group of four squadrons over distances and terrain he himself had never flown. Moreover, the weather was forecast to be marginal, with low visibility on the way to the target and uncertainty about whether they would be able to see the bridges at all.

Once they took off, Patterson discovered that the weather was even worse than forecast. The clouds were so thick that the ground was rarely visible. In and out of weather, the thirty-six pilots sometimes couldn't see one another's planes. Many might have aborted the mission. As group leader, it was Patterson's call. If he continued the mission, he could end up risking his group for no gain, because unless the target was visible, they couldn't hit it. Taking out the bridges was critical; over them flowed the weapons and munitions used to supply a numerically superior enemy that was advancing deep into South Korea.

"I'm sure at least a few of the pilots would have been just as happy if I had made the decision to turn back," Patterson recalls. "The weather increased the risks considerably, and we might get to the target area and still not be able to find the bridges. Still, it was worth the risk because of the tremendous problems our troops faced on the ground." As they flew on, the other pilots realized just how committed Patterson was to completing the mission, and it strengthened their own resolve.

Continues Patterson, "I flew a heading I had already planned on the ground. If the winds didn't change too much, and we maintained the airspeed I had previously calculated on the ground, we should get to the target area on schedule. Unfortunately, our navigation was made more difficult because we sometimes had to alter course due to poor weather conditions."

Good fortune smiled on Pat that day. His lead flight of four aircraft broke out of the clouds not far from the target. "I've got the bridges at eleven o'clock!" shouted Patterson's wingman over the intercom. (If you visualize a clock face with the airplane at its center pointing toward twelve o'clock, the wingman was saying that he had identified the bridges slightly off the nose of their aircraft to the left.)

"I was very much relieved," says Patterson. "The bridges were in plain sight, and we could hit them." He led the lead flight in a diving attack. Despite the fire of anti-aircraft guns, Patterson's flight dropped their bombs right on the target and knocked one span down. Banking sharply to the left and then back to the right as they climbed to avoid anti-aircraft fire, Patterson thought his flight's work was done and they could go home. He was wrong.

"As we began to reform out of the effective range of the anti-aircraft guns, we saw enemy MiG-15 fighters approaching rapidly. We barely had the fuel to return to base and we were no match for the MiGs. Moreover, combat maneuvering would eat up more fuel. However, if we didn't fight the MiGs, the rest of the Group would be in serious trouble. They would attack our guys just as they rolled in on the target. I had to make an immediate decision. If I stayed to fight, I would be betting the safe return of our four aircraft against our ability to fly through the weather and land safely with minimum fuel."

Patterson turned his flight to intercept the MiGs. At the same time he alerted the American F-86 "Sabres" that were flying top cover. Then he warned his other F-80s, which were just entering the target area. Patterson's pilots knew that with the delay in the flight's return, their chance of returning safely was diminished. However, because Patterson was extraordinarily committed, they were too.

"We opened fire while the MiGs were still out of range. The MiGs scattered and their leader made a very bad decision. They flew straight up—right into the waiting guns of the F-86s." Patterson's job in the target area was finally over, but his problems were not. "I could hardly keep my eyes off the fuel gauges all the way home." It was close, but everyone made it back.[2]

What made the entire group follow Patterson's lead unquestioningly, despite the risks? Pat had the experience—he knew what he was doing—but above all he displayed uncommon commitment. When the leader does this, others will do the same. They will follow. Thanks to Patterson's showing uncommon commitment, the bridges were destroyed and many American lives were saved.

On January 15, 2009, the world saw another flier with uncommon commitment save lives, but not in war. Chesley B. "Sully" Sullenberger III took off from La Guardia Airport in Manhattan, captain of US Airways flight 1549 bound for Charlotte, North Carolina. Almost immediately the plane ran into a flock of Canada geese, and both of the Airbus 320's engines quit. Sullenberger first sought to return to the airport, but he realized at once that he didn't have sufficient altitude. He then spotted another airfield, in New Jersey, but saw he had insufficient altitude to make that one either. With seconds to make a decision, Sullenberger didn't hesitate. He told the crew and passengers, "Prepare for ditching." You can count the number of successful ditchings of modern jet airliners, not on one hand but on one finger. That day, Captain Sullenberger not only successfully ditched his aircraft in the Hudson River he maintained a calm demeanor, which helped all 150 passengers survive the emergency landing with minimal injuries. The five crew members also survived. Sullenberger, by the way, had served as a U.S. Air Force fighter pilot from 1973 to 1980.[3]

Napoleon Bonaparte knew what these two fliers knew. In his *Maxims* he declared, "An extraordinary situation calls for extraordinary resolution. . . . How many things have appeared impossible which, nevertheless, have been done by resolute men."[4]

Commitment in Business

"Okay," you might say, "if the leader shows uncommon commitment in battle or in a dire emergency, it motivates. Followers echo the commitment of the leader, and the group has a much better chance of performing the task successfully. But that's not going to work in business, where people have distractions like their families, earning a living, or just having a good time. They've got to know they must perform—or else! The leader's showing uncommon commitment has nothing to do with it." Well, wait and see. It is my contention that extraordinary commitment motivates not only followers but others with whom the leader comes in contact: bosses, associates, moneylenders, and people far removed from the immediate organization. Pat Patterson's life offers another instance of the power of extraordinary commitment—this time in civilian life.

Patterson retired from the Air Force as a general. Later he became president of Ohio Precision Castings. The company contracted to supply a new type of fuel pump for the then new B-1 bomber. Several million dollars and many jobs were on the line.

As Patterson explains, "Molding these new pumps was no easy task. It had never been done before. No matter how carefully the molders worked, many of the pumps did not meet the specifications. There were so many rejects that we got behind schedule and were losing money. I was pretty worried."

Pat could have renegotiated the contract. He could have asked for a delay. He could have scaled back the number of units he was required to supply. All of these alternatives would have meant profitability but would have hurt the company's reputation and delayed production of the B-1. They would also have meant laying off some of his workers.

Others, faced with similar problems, did these things. Patterson didn't. Instead, he put everyone to work as they had never worked before. "I met repeatedly with the production crews and engineers. Everyone got into the spirit of solving the problem. I knew there had to be a solution and we tried all sorts of crazy things." Patterson's employees took note of his commitment. They saw he wasn't going to quit, so they didn't either. As his followers had done years earlier in the clouded skies over North Korea, his employees stuck with their leader.

Finally, Patterson's experts found something interesting. Since they were dealing with a single molding material, the formula and molding temperature for each part was normally the same as for all other parts; only the shape of the parts varied. However, this time the uniform approach wasn't working. Through experimentation, they found they could meet the specification by varying the temperature and formula for each part. One problem remained: it was not clear whether developing and using so many different casting formulas simultaneously was possible. It had never been done before. Some of Patterson's people concluded that this meant they could not succeed. One said, "Well, boss, I guess this means we've got to renegotiate the contract?"

Patterson thought otherwise. Because of his uncommon commitment, they kept at it. Everyone became obsessed with finding a solution. They not only worked overtime; they worked night and day. Eventually, they discovered the correct formula for each separate casting. "We posted it near the molding production machine for each part," Patterson recalls. As they molded each part differently, the number of rejects began to decline.

As it happened, they ran into yet another problem. Patterson's engineers found that air contacting the exterior of the aluminum molds caused the molding temperature to vary. Varying temperatures caused minor differences in the parts—minor but out of tolerance again. Consultants said that nothing could be done. Air always leaked around the exterior of the mold to some degree. "The specifications required," they maintained, "are just too tough."

Patterson wouldn't give up. Because he wouldn't give up, his workers wouldn't give up. "Finally, somebody came up with the idea of using ordinary plastic Saran Wrap to stop the air from escaping," Patterson says. "We tried it, and believe it or not it worked." Patterson got back on schedule and delivered the pumps on time—making a good profit and keeping his whole workforce on the job.[5]

Why don't more leaders in business do this? Jacques Naviaux was director of business planning at Hughes Aircraft Company. He is also a retired Marine Corps colonel who fought in combat in Vietnam. "In all too many circumstances, civilian leadership has been reluctant to make the extraordinary commitment required for sustained success," he explains.[6]

The Magic of Uncommon Commitment

What's so special about showing uncommon commitment? Why do others follow a leader who demonstrates this quality both on and off the battlefield? Psychologists have identified two main reasons why showing uncommon commitment yields such dramatic results:

It proves that the goal is worthwhile.

It proves that the leader isn't going to quit.

Followers Value the Goal

People don't exert themselves for little, unimportant goals. They work hard, take great risks, and let nothing stop them only for big, important goals. That's why leaders who try to play down the difficulty of a task make a big mistake. Those who practice Heroic Leadership know that it is far better to tell people exactly what is expected of them, no matter how serious the situation is or how much effort is required. Then, according to Walter "Buz" Baxter, president of the Baxter Seed Company of Weslaco, Texas, and formerly a major general in the Air Force, "you've got to hold everyone, including yourself, responsible for their own actions, and accept nothing less than their best effort."[7] That's the essence of showing uncommon commitment.

During the darkest days of World War II, Winston Churchill told his countrymen, "I have nothing to offer you but blood, sweat, toil, and tears." Churchill was 100 percent committed, and the British people knew it. Showing uncommon commitment proves that the goal is important enough to sacrifice for it.

Followers Match the Leader

People won't follow you if they think that your commitment is temporary or that you may quit short of attaining the goal. Why should they? Why should they invest their time, money, life, or fortune in something if the leader isn't going to lead them there in the end? Others will follow you, but only when they are convinced that you won't quit, no matter how difficult the task begins to look and no matter what obstacles you encounter along the way.

There will always be obstacles. It is true, as the saying goes, that "there are no dreams without dragons." When you demonstrate uncommon commitment, followers know that their investment of time and effort won't be wasted. They know that you won't walk away—that you will see the task through to the end. Yes, there will be dragons. But your uncommon commitment gives everyone confidence that, with you, they can and will slay them.

W. H. Tankersley was vice chairman of the board of directors of Sterne, Agee & Leach's investment banking in Montgomery, Alabama. He previously served as deputy assistant secretary of defense and had been a rifle and mortar platoon leader in combat during the Korean War. Tankersley continued to serve in the Army Reserve and retired as a major general. His advice: "If you want to inspire confidence in those you lead, you've got to have the commitment which expresses itself in physical and moral courage, and display both."[8] Do this, and those you lead will know that you won't quit.

If your team is convinced that the goal is important and that you are not going to stop until you reach that goal, then watch out! There is nothing they won't do to show you that their commitment is equal to yours, and nothing will stop them until they reach that goal or accomplish that task with you.

Changing the Face of an Industry

Irwin Jacobs, chairman of Qualcomm, cofounded his company to develop digital wireless technology in 1985. U.S. industry had adopted a system known as time-division multiple access (TDMA) as its digital standard. It had greater reliability than other systems, and this was considered the most important factor.

Jacobs stubbornly developed his products based on a less popular system called code-division multiple access (CDMA) based on compression technology. Jacobs was convinced that his system had far greater potential because of its increased access capacity. No wishy-washy "definite maybes" for Jacobs. He declared to everyone inside and outside the firm that this was the way they were going to proceed. He made a public commitment within and without his company and, regardless of development setbacks or criticism, continued to base his products on CDMA. It is very difficult to back down after you've made a public commitment, and everyone knew it. Jacobs was so committed that others stayed with him, even though some outsiders said he was nuts.

Four years later Jacobs approached the Cellular Telephone Industries Association (CTIA) to present his concepts. He had made compression technology work reliably. His timing could hardly have been worse: the CTIA had just waged its own internal fight over standards and technologies. The main competitor to TDMA was the general standard for mobile communications (GSM), the European standard. Jacobs's CDMA had not even been considered. The fight had been bitter, but TDMA had finally prevailed. That's when Jacobs wandered in with a proposal that they now consider CDMA. They wasted no time listening to Jacobs or a presentation on CDMA. According to Jacobs, "They threw us out on our ears."[9] But Jacobs didn't quit. Again, he publicly claimed that his compression technology would increase networks' capacity many times over that of other systems. He showed uncommon commitment while the entire industry ridiculed him and belittled his development. His supporters didn't desert him.

After two more years of struggle, he convinced the wireless division of Pacific Telesis to put up $2 million to build a trial network in San Diego. The results of the trial convinced the CTIA to do something it had once hoped to avoid: it reopened the standards debate. Two years later the CTIA approved CDMA as a second standard.

Contrary to helping Qualcomm's interest, reopening the standards debate almost caused the roof to fall in. Several corporations had already sunk millions in TDMA. They viciously attacked CDMA as too expensive, too complicated, and susceptible to jamming. Jacobs was even branded a fraud by these powerful self-interested groups.

Still, when you show such uncommon commitment, somehow others will continue to follow your leadership. That's what happened. Despite everything, two companies, Northern Telecom and Motorola, agreed to license Qualcomm's CDMA technology. Actually, their licensing didn't amount to much. They were simply covering their bets in case CDMA turned out to be real. Even so, it was a success of sorts for Qualcomm, and with this success Jacobs went to Asia to look for more business. His detractors tried everything to prevent additional sales. Letters were even sent to likely prospects warning of CDMA's problems and suggesting that CDMA be subjected to the closest scrutiny and that Jacobs's claims not be believed.

Objective testing began to support everything that Jacobs had said. Then came a major sales breakthrough. Major carriers of digital wireless, including PrimeCo and Sprint PCS, signed on to use CDMA technology. But even these adoptions created a problem. No one made CDMA handsets, and Sprint and PrimeCo needed tens of thousands of them. What to do now?

Not to worry. Remember, Jacobs was still publicly committed. He didn't falter. Instead, he convinced Sony to put up 49 percent in a joint phone-making venture. Qualcomm was now in the cellular phone business with a hefty multimillion-dollar order for phones, a product it hadn't even considered previously.

Even this success did not come without problems. There is a learning curve in manufacturing, and companies that have previously stuck to research and development invariably find they have lots of new challenges. A Qualcomm shipment of thousands of phones was halfway across the country as Jacobs tried desperately to meet a delivery deadline for Sprint. Suddenly it was discovered that each and every phone had a defective menu screen. The truck had to turn around and speed back to Qualcomm's plant in San Diego for rapid reprogramming.

That wasn't all. Ten days before PrimeCo's national rollout of its phones someone tried one of the buttons on a Qualcomm phone. An ear-piercing screech nearly deafened him. A second phone was tried with the same results. And then a third. Testing uncovered the problem; it was in the software. Every single phone had deafening screeches. With forty thousand phones already shipped, it was too late to ship them back to San Diego. Engineers had to fly out to PrimeCo's Florida warehouse with a just-in-time fix. It took four days to reprogram all forty thousand phones with help from every set of hands they could find to turn screws, open up the phones, and make the changes. Once again, they managed just barely to make the deadline.

Despite all the problems, showing uncommon commitment has its rewards. Most of the new generation wireless systems use Jacobs's CDMA technology, which continues to grow today.[10] Qualcomm revenues were more than $11 billion in 2008. The company has won numerous awards such as *Industry Week*'s 100 Best Managed Companies and *Fortune*'s 100 Best Companies to Work For in America.[11] Irwin Jacobs, chairman of Qualcomm, is still committed. And because he is committed, so is everyone else in his company. Today one of his sons is CEO and another is chief marketing officer.[12]

Commitment and Risk

Of course, commitment means taking risks. Some leaders are afraid to show uncommon commitment for this reason. To be frank, some are afraid to show any commitment at all. Yet risk is a part of life. Your willingness to accept risk is one of your responsibilities as leader. And accepting risk is one clear way of showing uncommon commitment.

How do Heroic Leaders learn to take risks every day? Simple. First they analyze the situation. Then they ask themselves, what is the worst that can happen? They assess whether the goal is worth risking the worst that can happen. If it is, they accept the risk and go ahead. Remarkable: once you accept the worst that can happen, you have much less difficulty accepting the risk. After that, you should have no difficulty making—and showing—an uncommon commitment.

Summary

It was General George S. Patton Jr. who said, "In case of doubt, push on just a little further and then keep on pushing." Heroic Leaders know that when you show uncommon commitment people will follow you toward any goal. To do this,

- Keep going when the going gets rough.
- Let people know it's a big tough job, not a little easy one.
- Make a public commitment.
- Accept the risk.

CHAPTER 5

• •

Expect Positive Results

• •

You can think positively, or negatively. It's your choice. However, most negative leaders do not expect positive results. On the contrary, they frequently expect the worst to happen—and it does. I don't know whether this is some kind of magic, but it doesn't matter. It's a fact: what we think of we get, whether it's positive or negative. It's not that the successful leaders I spoke with were Pollyannas. Some were iron-hard and steely-eyed realists. But that didn't stop them from thinking positively. And that made them expect to win.

What I noticed was that these positive thinkers kept their eyes on the prize (what they wanted, their goals, their tasks) and not on what they wanted to avoid. To do this, they would ask themselves, "What is the worst thing that can happen?" They would assess the risk, and if it was acceptable they would plunge ahead and do what needed to be done.

Do you think that someone who has already considered the worst that can happen, accepted it, even planned what action to take if worst does come to worst is less fearful and thinks more positively? You bet! No wonder such individuals expect to win. Of course, the definition of "winning" may be much broader than succeeding with the immediate task. Some efforts which appear to be unsuccessful in the immediate goal have longer-range effects, some of which cannot be anticipated at the time. The "three hundred Spartans" failed to stop the attacking Persians under Xerxes at Thermopylae in the late summer of 480 B.C., and the defending Spartans perished to the last man. But the effort united the Greek states and inspired them to ultimate victory—much as the Texans' stand at the Alamo did more than two thousand years later.

• • • •

On the evening of March 3, 2002, Senior Chief Petty Officer Britt Slabinski led his seven-man SEAL reconnaissance team via helicopter onto the snow-covered, 10,000-foot mountaintop known as Takur Ghar, to establish a position in support of U.S. Army forces advancing against the enemy on the valley floor. His unit was conducting combat operations against the Taliban during Operation Anaconda in the Sahi-Kot Valley, Afghanistan, in support of Operation Enduring Freedom. As their helicopter hovered over the mountain, it was met by sudden rocket-propelled grenade (RPG) and small-arms fire from entrenched enemy forces. As a result of several RPG hits, a member of Slabinski's team was blown from the helicopter right into the midst of the enemy's positions. The badly damaged helicopter made a controlled crash. Senior Chief Slabinski immediately established security at the crash site and organized his remaining team members and the aircrew. They were evacuated by another helicopter to a support base. But Britt Slabinski wasn't done. He was fully aware of the overwhelming enemy forces on the mountain, but he also knew that his missing team member was alive and fighting for his life. He decided to go back for the man. Because he expected positive results, his men willingly followed him back to the danger zone.

Mounting a fresh helicopter, they headed for the snow-covered mountaintop despite the numerically superior enemy forces that dominated it. After a dangerous helicopter insertion of the SEAL team onto the mountaintop, Slabinski led his small band into a close-quarter firefight. He attacked multiple enemy positions, personally clearing one bunker and killing the enemies within. But the team became caught in a withering crossfire from other bunkers and from advancing forces. Several of the team were hit. An extremely difficult situation emerged. Some might have thought of surrendering, but Slabinski expected to win. Collecting his wounded, he led a difficult movement through the mountainous terrain; constantly under fire, they covered over one kilometer in waist-deep snow to a defensible position. There he reorganized the team and took care of his wounded. Slabinski directed the defense of this position through continuous attacks until, with air support, the enemy was totally defeated. Senior Chief Petty Officer Slabinski had saved the lives of his wounded men that day, and even with being outnumbered had defeated the enemy and captured Takur Ghar. He was able to do all this because he had no doubt. In the end he was unable to rescue the team member he had sought to help. But like the Spartans and the Texans before him he had expected to win, and in the larger view, he did.[1]

It is true that a leader who expects all positive results may not actually get them, as in the case of Petty Officer Slabinski. Sometimes external circumstances can't be controlled. But it is equally true that a leader who does not expect positive results will get little if anything in this direction. So, while expecting positive results may not always lead to success, failing to expect positive results will almost always lead to failure. As General Colin Powell says, "Perpetual optimism is a force multiplier."[2]

Salvaging Success in Antiquity

It was more than forty years ago that Peter Drucker advised reading what he called "the first systematic book on leadership" in his own book *The Practice of Management*.[3] He was referring to some of the writings of Xenophon, a Greek general who wrote several books about battle leadership. Drucker proclaimed that all the latest research was nothing compared to what had already been written on the subject more than two millennia ago. One of Xenophon's books was *Anabasis*, a title one source translates as *Expedition Up Country*.[4] In 401 B.C., Xenophon led ten thousand Greek soldiers in retreat from Persia to the Greek Black Sea colony of Trapezus—a distance of more than a thousand miles. They faced an enemy who was greatly superior in numbers, and they were continually opposed by unfriendly tribes throughout the five-month march.

Some months earlier Cyrus the Younger, son of Cyrus the Great, had enlisted these troops to help him overthrow his brother, Artaxerxes, who was king of Persia. At the Battle of Cunaxa they fought a Persian army many times their size. In the midst of the battle, Cyrus was killed. Even so, the Greek general Clearchus, who was second in command, changed front, advanced against the right wing of the Persian army, and for all practical purposes won the battle.

But since Cyrus, the pretender to the Persian throne, was dead, there was little point to the victory of his troops. In fact the Persians in Cyrus's army deserted to Artaxerxes, who told the Greeks that with Cyrus dead there was no reason for their continuing to fight. To use two clichés in one sentence, he was willing to "forgive and forget" and to "live and let live." He offered a truce, and the Greek mercenaries accepted it. Artaxerxes told them they could return to their own country unhindered. To celebrate the truce, he invited the Greek generals to a great banquet. They were told to leave their weapons outside. Once they were unarmed, Artaxerxes had them all killed. He then offered a truce to the Greek army, which was now without senior leaders.

Xenophon had been a young staff officer. He gathered the surviving officers together, and under his guidance they elected new generals. Xenophon was elected general in chief. Now some of his officers wanted to open up a dialogue with Artaxerxes. They saw no way of marching such a great distance through unfriendly country and were discouraged by the numerically superior Persian army that faced them. Xenophon knew that given the chance, Artaxerxes would kill them as he had killed their leaders. He assembled the officers and spoke to them. "All of these soldiers have their eyes on you, and if they see that you are downhearted they will become cowards, while if you are yourselves clearly prepared to meet the enemy and if you call on the rest to do their part, you can be sure that they will follow you and try to be like you."[5]

Xenophon expected positive results. Even though they had lost their experienced and proven generals, were numerically inferior to their enemy, had over a thousand miles of unfriendly territory to traverse, and lacked supplies of food and water, he convinced his fellow officers and the rest of the army that they would return to their homes. Because Xenophon expected positive results, his ten thousand followers expected positive results as well. The Greek army escaped from Artaxerxes and followed Xenophon on the most amazing march in history. They completed their journey successfully despite countless battles and hardships. No wonder Drucker called our attention to Xenophon's work as containing important lessons for leading in business.

Rescuing a Modern Company

Expecting positive results can work miracles in business. Supercuts was a revolutionary concept in the 1970s when it was introduced. It replaced the old barbershop and beauty shop with low-cost, no-nonsense unisex hairstyling salons. Supercuts was extremely successful. It grew and its franchises expanded across the country. However, at some point its leaders grew fearful. Dreading the loss of all they had gained, they no longer expected positive results.

According to Major General Hoyt S. Vandenberg Jr., USAF, retired, all leaders fall into two groups: the hunters and the hunted. Hunted leaders are trying to avoid failure; in their hearts they lack self-confidence and don't expect to succeed. Hunter leaders expect to win. They are enthusiastically hunting success—and they fully expect to find it.[6]

Once hunters, Supercuts' leaders became the hunted. They began to fear the worst. As frequently happens when leaders are fearful, Supercuts' fears began to materialize. This was probably due to the leaders' own actions. In attempting to protect profits, they started to save money by cutting corners. As a result, franchisees felt short-changed in advertising and other support, and relations between them and the corporation grew cool. The franchisees formed an association to protect their interests. Corporate leaders attempted to keep them from doing this. This led to a class-action lawsuit against the corporation.

By 1987 Supercuts was in deep trouble. Sales were down; morale was low; the company was floundering. Some business watchers were predicting bankruptcy. At the last minute, an investment company bought the company and brought in a new CEO. Her name was Betsy Burton, and she was a Heroic Leader.

Burton met with the franchisees even before the deal went through. They were so impressed with her openness and positive expectations that they dropped the lawsuit without her even asking. Why? Previously, the franchisees had asked to set up a joint council with company management. Supercuts' old leaders wouldn't even consider it. They knew it was a good idea, but they were afraid to be thought of as agreeing with the franchisees. Burton not only agreed; she offered to hold all meetings at corporate expense. She took these actions because she knew who she was and what she believed in—and she was unafraid to show it. Burton expected to succeed. She expected profits to go up, not down.

Within sixteen months profits were up by 10 percent. Within three years franchisees were enjoying double-digit sales increases. Revenue grew from $126 million to over $170 million. The corporation added more than one hundred new franchises.[7] Franchisees, employees, management—all were now expecting positive results. Betsy Burton, who always expected positive results, had expected them first.

Career Success Despite All Odds

One of the most positive-thinking military men I have ever met is Colin Powell, former chairman of the Joint Chiefs of Staff (JCS), which is the highest position in the U.S. military. I met General Powell when he addressed the *Los Angeles Times* Management Conference in March 1993, before he retired from that position. I found General Powell to be positive and upbeat. I was surprised at his high energy that day; his executive officer told me that it was his third speech that day, after speaking in San Antonio and San Francisco. Here it was, three o'clock in the afternoon, his third speech in cities hundreds of miles apart, and he showed no sign of fatigue.

Everyone knew he was in for some tough questioning. One of President Bill Clinton's campaign promises involved the issue of gays in the military. The rumor was that the joint chiefs had convinced the president to adopt a compromise position. There were other issues. Why couldn't the military budget be cut more, and faster? What was the future of the National Guard? Many were unhappy with the way the Army National Guard round-out brigades appear to have been treated during the Gulf War. Powell was facing the media in the heart of the enemy camp. He could be in for a rough time. But Powell gave a five-star speech. His positive thinking won over every one of the three hundred or so senior managers.

Yet Powell's career had not progressed without difficulty. His was not an "affirmative action success story," as some have suggested. There was real live bigotry and prejudice as Colin Powell rose through the ranks. There was no quota system to assist him. Powell made it to the very pinnacle of the U.S. Armed Forces on his own merit, sheer guts, and an incredibly positive attitude. Those whom General Powell led became positive thinkers because he was a positive thinker. That attitude culminated in his leading the armed forces during the most successful major military action since World War II.

While still chairman General Powell spoke to kids in the inner cities. And because he couldn't reach them all, he had ten thousand videotapes made and sent to high schools across the country. Here's what General Powell told the students:

> There's nothing you can't accomplish if you're willing to put your mind to it, if you're willing to set aside the negative influences that are out there, if you believe in yourself, if you're committed to yourself, and if you believe in this country, and if you let nothing hold you back.
>
> Don't let the fact that you're Hispanic or black or any other attribute hold you back. Just go for it. I did it; you can do it. Don't look for a silver bullet. Don't look for "a role model I'm going to follow." Be your own role model. Believe in yourself.[8]

Today we know that President Barack Obama followed Colin Powell's advice. He won the presidency even though he had gone up against others having far more "name recognition" and experience. But Barack Obama said, "Yes, we can!" and despite the odds against him, he went on to victory to become the forty-fourth president of the United States.

Visualize Success

If you want to learn to expect positive results, you've first got to see those results achieved in your own mind. Psychologists call this "mental visualization," and it is amazing what can be done with it. Mental visualization seems to work best in a very relaxed state; I have witnessed as well as been involved in a number of experiments that illustrate the power of this technique.

My wife is a clinical psychologist, and I have studied psychology at the graduate level. As a consequence, I've attended a number of seminars on hypnosis, many with her. Under a hypnotic trance, a subject is extremely relaxed and open to suggestion. One sequence involves having the subject picture himself standing in a lemon grove, picking a lemon, slicing it in half, and sucking up a bit of juice.

The surprising thing is that when subjects do this, their lips invariably pucker as they imagine the sweet-sour juice from the lemon in their mouth. One theory is that all hypnosis is really self-hypnosis, and to become entranced is quite easy. In fact, if you found yourself puckering your lips when you thought about the lemon juice, you did it yourself! But there is more. While in a hypnotic trance, a subject, after some visualization techniques, can be told that something about to touch bare skin is red hot. Believe it or not, an ice cube will actually raise a blister!

An even more amazing story about the power of mental visualization, especially regarding its use in expecting positive results, comes from psychologist Charles Garfield. I first read about Garfield in an article in the *Wall Street Journal* in January 1982. The article said that through visualization techniques, specifically through visualizing a positive outcome, Garfield was able to significantly increase the speaking performance of top executives. Later, Garfield wrote a book, *Peak Performers*, in which he described the following incident.

At a conference on peak performance in Milan, Italy, Garfield met some Russian scientists who began to discuss their current work. Discovering that Garfield was an amateur weightlifter, they invited him to participate in an experiment. The scientists learned that Garfield had been able to bench-press 280 pounds. They asked him the most he thought he could do; Garfield told them 300 pounds. After some encouragement, Garfield pressed 300 pounds. However, the press was made with great difficulty, and it required every ounce of his strength and concentration to do it.

Next the Russians put Garfield into a relaxed state and took him through a series of visualization exercises. During these exercises, he was told to visualize himself lifting 365 pounds, which to Garfield seemed utterly impossible. However, after an hour or so of the visualization process, not only was he able to make this difficult lift, but he felt it was far easier to make than the 300-pound lift he had done earlier![9] Visualizing success is an important part of expecting positive results. But it's not only important—it works!

Be Real

You can't be someone you are not. But the reality is that it makes no difference who you are. We're all different, but we all have the potential to be competent, even outstanding, leaders. Too many leaders try to be what they are not. They may in fact be kind and thoughtful yet afraid to display these qualities. They may have read management books that extolled a tough leadership style, so they want to be seen as tough. Or maybe they heard that the "new leader" has a participatory style. So they strive to encourage followers' participation even when it is inappropriate. Perhaps they try to be overly friendly when by nature they are more reserved.

Dick Leavitt flew in combat in Korea and was a wing commander in Vietnam. He retired from the Air Force as a lieutenant general and as vice commander of the Strategic Air Command. After retiring, he became senior vice president of Cessna Aircraft Company, and then president of other corporations. On thinking through some questions I had posed about combat leadership, he added, "After watching many units perform in and out of combat, I have concluded that a leader must be himself. It is less important whether a leader is authoritarian or participative. Assuming what a leader is not is very dangerous because stress will usually cause a leader to revert to his 'natural' personality. When that happens, his followers become unsure of him and quickly lose confidence."[10]

Maintain Your Enthusiasm

If you as leader aren't enthusiastic about something, no one else will be. That's a fact. You can't expect followers to enthusiastically accept a challenge that you haven't enthusiastically accepted yourself. Some say that one reason for the failure of Confederate general George Pickett's charge at Gettysburg was that his superior, General James Longstreet, lacked enthusiasm for making the attack. Longstreet had tried everything to dissuade General Robert E. Lee from ordering the charge, but he was unsuccessful. Having earlier given General Pickett a warning order, Longstreet was leaning dejectedly against a fence railing when Pickett came to him to receive the order to proceed.

"General, shall I advance?" asked Pickett, saluting. Longstreet returned the salute, but his head bowed and he said nothing. Pickett repeated his request. Still not getting a response, he asked, "If it is your desire that I proceed, nod your head." Longstreet, head still bowed, nodded in the affirmative. Pickett's charge, certainly the most gallant in history, was also one of the most costly—and it failed. Out of 10,500 who made the advance, only 4,830 came back to Confederate lines unscathed.[11]

Moving closer to the present day, in December 1950 the Chinese crossed the border into Korea in overwhelming numbers. U.N. forces under General Douglas MacArthur withdrew to avoid capture. Colonel "Chesty" Puller led a regiment of U.S. Marines in retreat from the Chinese border to the port of Hungnam in North Korea. It was the bitter cold of winter, but the Marines had only their summer uniforms. They had wounded to carry with them; their food supply was limited; and they had gone for days with little sleep. Yet Puller was upbeat and positive. He told his troops:

"You're the First Marine Division, and don't you forget it. We're the greatest military outfit that ever walked on this earth. Not all the communists in hell can stop you. We'll go down to the sea at our own pace and nothing is going to get in our way. If it does, we'll blow the hell out of it."

Puller got his regiment to the port of Hungnam successfully. From there it was evacuated to fight another day. Puller eventually retired from the Marines with the three stars of a lieutenant general. Puller is also the only man in U.S. military history to win the Navy Cross (the decoration that is second only to the Congressional Medal of Honor) *five* times! Puller knew how to maintain his enthusiasm and expect positive results.

I have found that if I'm not initially enthusiastic about a project, I can get worked up about it if it makes sense. Once I am excited and enthusiastic, I automatically expect positive results. How do I work myself up? I think of all the good things that will happen when I complete the project, and before long I find that I really am enthusiastic. From then on, I expect positive results.

Summary

If you want people to expect to win, then you must do so first. If you expect positive results, others will as well. To expect positive results as a leader,

- Become a positive thinker.
- Visualize the results you want to achieve.
- Be real.
- Maintain your enthusiasm.

CHAPTER 6

• •

Take Care of Your People

• •

Take care of your men and they will take care of you," says retired Brigadier General Philip Bolte, who served in combat in armored vehicles in both Korea and Vietnam. His remark echoes the sentiments of combat leaders back to Xenophon's time and doubtless beyond.[1] Thomas Noel, who fought in Vietnam and left the Army to assume a senior executive post in the Department of Energy and who later became president of a succession of companies, puts it even more bluntly: "Believe in your people and take care of them. You are what your people are, no more, and no less."[2]

But who are your people? Most think of "your people" as those you supervise directly, either on a temporary or a permanent basis. However, that is not necessarily the whole truth. In business, "your people" include your customers. The Chinese managers who allowed milk contaminated with industrial chemicals to be sold killed infants and put babies in danger all over the world through their exports.[3] The same was true of the managers of the American plant in Georgia who knowingly shipped peanut butter contaminated with salmonella to customers.[4] These are blatant instances of failure to meet even minimal standards in taking care of customers. At the same time, they are the worst examples of flouting the leadership law discussed in Chapter Seven: duty before self.

• • • •

On March 23, 2003, Hospital Apprentice Luis Fonseca, a Navy corpsman, was serving in a Marine amphibious assault vehicle platoon during an attack on the Saddam Canal Bridge in Iraq. An amphibious assault vehicle was struck by a rocket-propelled grenade and set on fire. The five Marines inside were wounded. Corpsman Fonseca braved small arms, machine gun, and intense grenade fire to rush to the vehicle, evacuate the wounded Marines, and tend to their wounds. He established a casualty collection point inside the unit's medical evacuation vehicle and stabilized two of the casualties who had serious, life-threatening injuries. He continued to treat and care for all the wounded while awaiting evacuation. Suddenly, the vehicle was hit and immobilized by enemy fire. Under a hail of machine gun bullets, Fonseca organized litter teams and directed the movement of four casualties from the damaged vehicle. He personally carried one critically wounded Marine over open ground to another vehicle. At this point the whole unit came under an artillery barrage. Fonseca again exposed himself to treat the Marines wounded in this attack. Returning to the newly designated casualty evacuation vehicle, he accompanied the wounded to a battalion aid station. After briefing medical personnel on the status of each patient, he returned to the battle to treat Marines who had been wounded in his absence.

Taking care of "his people" that day saved the lives of many Marines.[5] They obeyed his every order because they knew that he cared more for their safety than he did for his own—a living illustration of Xenophon's millennia-old observation: "People are only too glad to obey the man who they believe takes wiser thoughts for their interests than they themselves do."

How Far to Go

How far should you go in taking care of your people? Fortunately, your civilian career won't normally require you to lay down your life for your people in order to take care of them. But make no mistake: you must be willing to "go to the mat" for your people if you expect them to follow you to the same extent as they would a successful battle leader.

Dave Whitmore was an IBM marketing manager for a new region in New York that serviced utilities and telephone companies. The two largest accounts in Dave's area were in the care of two of his most senior marketing team leaders. These accounts represented a considerable amount of money, and the pressure was incredible. If any of IBM's computers in his region went down, Whitmore could lose his job.

One day Whitmore became aware of a serious problem. Neither one of his senior team leaders had ever held a staff job. He was told that if they weren't assigned to staff positions outside of his organization within the next few months, there was a good chance they would never get them. And if they never got staff jobs, their futures at IBM were limited. It would be unlikely they could ever get promoted to more senior positions. These were talented, hard-working people—their timing was just bad.

Whitmore talked it over with his two team leaders. He explained the situation to them. What did they want to do? Both expressed a willingness to stay if they had to, but both understood the necessity for obtaining staff experience. Both wanted to go. Whitmore was inexperienced in his new job. He had no other experienced team leaders, and none would be available if he let these two go. It was Whitmore's decision. Whitmore's boss, a branch manager, counseled him. "Who cares whether they become managers or not? It's your fanny on the line. If you let them go, you're taking a chance on losing everything you've worked for. Screw up, and I can't guarantee whether you can ever become a branch manager. Your sending them to staff positions may help them, but it may limit your future in the company." But Whitmore knew what he had to do. It was his responsibility to take care of his people. He saw that both team leaders were offered staff positions in IBM immediately. They both accepted and left his organization.

What happened to Dave Whitmore? He made do without his team leaders. Later, because of his success at this job, he was offered what he called his "dream job": international account manager in Brussels.[6]

When Things Go Wrong

When the chips are down and times are difficult, those who follow you really watch to see what you do. Do you really take care of your people, or is it all for show? Taking care of your people is made more difficult when it conflicts with other laws, directives, and orders. The leader must use careful judgment to discern between compromising other requirements, such as carrying out instructions from higher authority, and taking care of the people being led.

Harry G. Summers, a former Army colonel turned syndicated columnist, wrote that the commander has a responsibility "to shield his subordinate leaders from arbitrary and capricious attack."[7] Summers once illustrated this point by describing a combat action in Vietnam in which he was involved. Brigadier General James F. Hollingsworth (an assistant division commander) was flying over Summers's battle position in a helicopter. He called Summers's battalion commander, Lieutenant Colonel Dick Prillaman, on the radio and told him that one of his company commanders was all screwed up. "I want you to relieve him right now," he demanded. ("Relieve" is the military way of saying "fire.") That would have ended the company commander's career, but if he was "screwed up" and endangering his men or the mission, he had to be relieved. However, this was not the case. Hollingsworth only knew what he saw from the air. He wasn't on the ground and didn't know the whole story. Prillaman responded instantly, "He's doing exactly what I want him to do. If you relieve anyone, it should be me." General Hollingsworth could have done exactly that. Instead, he said, "Now dammit Dick, don't get your back up. It just looked screwed up from up here. Go down and check it out." By the time he retired from the Army, Prillaman was a lieutenant general.[8] Good leaders who take care of their people frequently get promoted. But not always.

Risking Prison

One June 2, 1967, two American F-105 pilots on a mission over Hanoi came under attack by guns protecting a ship unloading its military cargo in Haiphong Harbor. This was in an area which Secretary of Defense McNamara had essentially declared to be a sanctuary for the enemy. The ship, and the area surrounding it, could not be attacked under the American "rules of engagement." To save themselves, the two pilots instinctively fired back. They didn't stop to identify the ship, because there wasn't time. They simply opened fire to get away. The whole incident took less than five seconds. But the consequences could have been severe. It turned out that the ship unloading munitions for North Vietnam was a Russian freighter.

The commander responsible for these pilots was a colonel by the name of Jack Broughton. Broughton was on the fast track to make general. He was a graduate of one of the most prestigious senior service schools in the armed forces. He was smart, aggressive, and an outstanding leader. While many senior officers flew an occasional mission but spent much of their time behind a desk, Broughton scheduled himself to fly every tough mission. If there was a difficult combat mission over North Vietnam, you could bet Broughton was on it taking the same risks as his men.

When the strike force returned from the mission, the flight leader asked to see Broughton in private and told him what had happened. As Broughton commented, "That made it my problem." Complicating the matter was the fact that bad weather had forced the two pilots to land first at another American base. Still somewhat punchy from combat and frightened by the potential consequences of the attack they had made, which they knew were extremely serious, one of the pilots had signed a statement that he had not fired his guns. Broughton and his pilots knew that signing this report constituted a false official statement. Under military law, this in itself could lead to a dishonorable discharge even if made under the pressures of the moment and without time to reflect.

As Broughton said later, "This was not an easy decision nor was it made lightly."[9] The only evidence against the two pilots was the film from their own gun cameras. Broughton took the film and exposed it to a truck's headlights. Then he burned it. Broughton was not in favor of violating orders; however, he believed that while what these pilots had done was wrong, it was understandable and forgivable. Moreover, he knew that in this particular war such mistakes were not forgiven. Pilots violating the rules of engagement in the past had been punished severely for far lesser mistakes. But Broughton had been raised in an environment that said you take care of your people. He made the decision that if anyone was going to be punished over this incident, he would be the one, and not the two pilots.

As a result of Broughton's actions no one could prove which pilots had been involved in the incident. Broughton was court-martialed. He freely admitted burning the film. He was found guilty, fined, and admonished—and sentenced to a military prison. On appeal, a board of high-ranking civilians from the Office of the Secretary of the Air Force set the prison term aside. But his career was ended, and obviously he was never promoted to general.

Broughton wrote two best-selling books, *Thud Ridge* and *Going Downtown*, and more recently an autobiography, *Rupert Red Two*. On Broughton's last combat mission over North Vietnam, one of the pilots he had protected saved his life. As Jack Broughton told me in an interview some years ago, "That's a type of poetic justice and in a real sense made it all worthwhile."[10]

Were Broughton's actions in destroying the gun camera film right or wrong? I don't know. You have to make your own call. The point I want to make is just how far this leader went in taking care of his people. He was willing to sacrifice his career, even go to jail if necessary, to protect them from what he felt would be unduly harsh and unjust punishment for an error made under fire. The ship, by the way, had been supplying the enemy with ground-to-air missiles.

How ignoble this makes the actions of some leaders look! Some of these so-called leaders go so far as to blame subordinates when things go wrong. Others think nothing about inconveniencing those they lead; they are untroubled by their employees' working conditions or whether their work schedules are causing family hardships, and they have no reservations about firing them to cut costs and bolster the bottom line. As far as they are concerned, their people are so much fodder for the system; any subordinate who doesn't like it can go elsewhere! Is it any wonder that these corporate executives are not considered leaders by those they purport to lead?

Learning Priorities

If you are the leader, you've got to learn to give the needs of those you lead greater weight than you give your personal needs. Again, you must balance this with your mission, which has to come first. This sometimes makes for a difficult judgment call. Is it the mission you are primarily concerned with in putting aside your people's needs, or is it your own needs? If it's really your own needs, and taking care of your people makes your job just a little tougher or a little riskier, then maybe you had better think again.

Before joining IBM, Dave Whitmore had been an Air Force captain serving as navigator of one of Strategic Air Command's B-52 nuclear bombers during the height of the Cold War. When the Vietnam War heated up, SAC crews rotated duty flying combat missions out of Guam with nonnuclear weapons. That heated things up even more. Whitmore flew several rounds of these combat tours and received training to go to a nuclear war. Even though he spent so much time on his job flying, his real interest was in engineering. When he had first volunteered for flying duties, he anticipated a couple years "in the cockpit" before being sent for an advanced degree in engineering and then applying this knowledge to aviation problems. However, shortly after Whitmore completed his training, the Air Force more than doubled the amount of time a new flier had to remain flying. Even so, he took tests and qualified for the Air Force's master's program in astronautics.

Unfortunately, unit commanders were under considerable pressure not to release fliers to advanced degree programs. Every trained SAC crewman replaced by one with less experience meant more difficulties for his commander. Since promotions for commanders were highly competitive and crews were constantly being tested, there was no question that Whitmore's loss would represent a significant career risk to his commander, and to commanders at higher organizational levels. Would Whitmore's commander allow him to leave SAC to get his degree?

Said Whitmore, "Despite the personal downside to my bosses, my commander supported me 100 percent. He told me, 'Dave, if you wait around until the time is perfect for us you will never get your master's degree. That's important to the Air Force, too!'" Whitmore left SAC and entered a master's program. Later, Captain Whitmore discovered that it hadn't been so simple: a higher leader had tried to block his transfer for graduate training. But Whitmore's immediate commander had dug his heels in and stuck his neck out, guaranteeing no drop in crew performance despite Whitmore's leaving. Whitmore realized that his commander had taken risks for his sake.

He had placed Whitmore's needs above his own, and Whitmore vowed to do the same as a leader himself; and as we saw previously, he did.

Taking Personal Responsibility

Every combat leader I talked to spoke about the importance of taking personal responsibility for his actions and for the actions of his organization. Whenever something went right, these leaders gave credit to their people. But when things didn't go right, they took personal responsibility. Most of the time this was done simply, in the manner of General Lee after the failure of Pickett's Charge at the Battle of Gettysburg. Lee told everyone, "It's all my fault." He took personal responsibility for the defeat. Sometimes, taking personal responsibility must be expressed in the physical sense; that is, the heroic leader must take actions for the benefit of others that he knows will damage his own well-being, such as in the case of Colonel Broughton. At other times, it's in the moral sense. It means taking personal responsibility because you are the leader. It may not hurt you in a physical sense, though it may damage your reputation. That's what General Lee did. The practitioners of Heroic Leadership do either, or both, in taking care of their people.

Summary

To be a Heroic Leader, you must take care of the people who report to you. If you look after your people, they will perform to their maximum capability. If you fail to do this, you won't be their leader for very long. To make sure you are taking care of those who follow you,

- Be the leader when things go wrong.
- Give your people's needs priority.
- Really care.
- Take responsibility.

CHAPTER 7

• •

Put Duty Before Self

• •

Not atypically, if you look up *duty* in the dictionary, you will find several definitions. Two definitions help capture the sense of what this universal law of Heroic Leadership requires: 1. The actions required by one's occupation or position; 2. A moral or legal obligation.

• • • •

When General H. Norman Schwarzkopf was Major Schwarzkopf, he served as an adviser to a South Vietnamese brigade. One of the senior Vietnamese officers was a colonel by the name of Ngo Quang Truong. Colonel Truong was short and skinny and didn't look like a military hero. Still, he was worshiped by his troops and feared by the enemy commanders who knew about him. During a mission to find and destroy an enemy unit, Truong and Schwarzkopf were leading in an armored command vehicle. Suddenly, a hidden machine gun fired and Schwarzkopf was hit.

"I was in a little bit of shock as the medic bandaged me up," Schwarzkopf said. "Truong squatted beside me and said, 'My friend, if you would like, I will turn the personnel carrier around, and we will go back and get you a medevac. But I don't want to do that. We're in the position we need to be in, and I need your help.'"

Schwarzkopf agreed to keep going. They attacked using a plan Schwarzkopf had helped develop. Truong's troops saw that Schwarzkopf put duty first. So they did the same. The result was a complete rout of enemy forces.[1]

Duty First

Duty before self is a law of leadership that is as true in the boardroom as the battlefield. It is a critical part of Heroic Leadership.

Harry Walters is one of those unusual leaders whose experience spans the Army, the civilian world, and government service. After graduating from West Point and serving three years in the Army, he went into industry. He worked himself up to marketing manager of a company, then vice president, and finally president. At that point, President Reagan asked him to enter government service as assistant secretary of the Army and, two years later, as Veterans Administration Administrator. Leaving government, Walters became CEO of several corporations.

Reflecting on his very heavy intercollegiate sports background—in football, basketball, and baseball—he says, "I always felt I was playing in a team environment whether in government or industry. If that environment didn't exist, I always felt it was my job to create it. That's the only way to win. If you don't put duty before self, you can't create a team environment.

"Unfortunately, that was the situation at the Veterans Administration at first. A team environment just didn't exist. No one put duty first. There was a $30 billion budget to take care of eleven million veterans, and it seemed that too many were looking out for themselves and protecting their own turf. Lincoln had started the Veterans Administration 'to care for him that has born the battle.' By the early eighties, it seemed that Lincoln's philosophy had got lost somewhere, and it was as if the purpose of the VA was to restrict the benefits to which veterans were supposedly entitled, and to make things as tough as possible for them. The VA had taken on an adversarial role to veterans when it should have been an advocacy role. Moreover, there was no mission statement, no planning, no nothing.

"To me, duty before self means inclusion with no secrets. Why should there be any secrets, when the leader puts his own interests last? So I brought everybody into the party. That meant the veterans organizations like the American Legion, the Veterans of Foreign Wars, and the Jewish War Veterans; Congress, who both represented the veterans and in addition were our bankers; and even the press. I held a press conference every Monday morning. When things went wrong, the press didn't need to call me, I called them. I think I was one of the few people in government who the press never harassed."

"I gave the VA employees a mission: to help vets, with no politics and no secrets from anyone. Duty before self meant that the well-being of the veteran came before any individual in the VA. We measured progress and held everyone accountable. We developed a motto, 'America Is Number One Thanks to Our Veterans.' When people realized this was for real, we got cooperation from everyone, from both parties in the U.S. Congress to the media. The VA employees were superb."

"Industry is no different. I spent a lot of time with unions. But not fighting with them. I wanted them to understand my perception and I began to understand theirs. We spent far more time on how we could master the environment than we did with complaints. And in my opinion, that's the way it should be. We were both on the same side. If there was 'an enemy,' it was the competition, not me, and not them. When a leader puts duty before self, he helps to create that team environment—whether it's government or private industry—that is absolutely essential for success."[2]

A Rarity in Industry

Is the attitude displayed by these heroes common in industry? Unfortunately, no. In many companies the automatic solution to any slip in profits or in the stock market is downsizing. *Newsweek* states, "After causing the problems through poor decisions, many CEOs offer up their employees as human sacrifices, hoping to get their stock prices up. If they do go up, they get a raise even while their employees suffer."[3]

The *Newsweek* article may have overstated the case. For example, it did not sufficiently emphasize that when workers are doing jobs that are no longer needed, or corporate survival is at stake, it is the leader's duty to take action, which may include layoffs. Otherwise, the company will ultimately fail, and no one will have work. However, the article correctly made the following points, which no corporate leader should ignore:

- A leader does not use people as corporate fodder simply to look better on the bottom line.

- A leader does everything possible, when people must be released from their work, to assist and prepare them for their future.

- A leader takes personal cuts before laying off anyone, and shares the pain by taking more personal cuts if layoffs are unavoidable.

- A leader never benefits by the misfortunes of those being led.

Not all American managers treat workers "as a tool to make money." But some do. The leaders the *Newsweek* article talked about did not put duty before self. They transposed the correct order of priorities and put their own welfare before the needs of those they led. They fired loyal, productive workers, not for corporate survival but merely to make profits look better. They did little or nothing to prepare or help those who had to leave the company. They actually accepted salary increases and bonuses while increasing the misery of those who had trusted in them and followed them. This is not duty before self, and it is certainly not Heroic Leadership.

Mission and People

Combat leaders know that concern for mission and concern for people are closely intertwined, since without people you cannot accomplish the mission; they cannot be considered separately. If you adopt the priorities of mission or people in any fixed order, it will eventually be wrong for a particular situation.

The notion that you must have high concern for both mission and people may have originated in combat leadership, but it has been confirmed by management researchers. In *The Managerial Grid* and *The New Managerial Grid* Robert Blake and Jane Mouton describe a system of managerial effectiveness through a matrix showing concern for production on one axis and concern for people on the other. In a day when management books were only just gaining in popularity, their first book, published in 1964, sold almost a million copies. Their conclusions sound almost self-evident today: a leader's high concern both for production and for people ("head and heart," they called it) leads to a number of beneficial and synergistic consequences.[4]

To follow the concepts of Heroic Leadership, you must consider both people and mission as very important, but not in a fixed priority. At times the top priority must be given to mission or work. At other times your people must be given top priority. As a leader you must keep both at the top of your list and judge which gets the primary call in a specific situation. Both, of course, must come before self.

Consider Yourself Last

Sure, you've got to consider yourself. You owe something to yourself, and you have responsibilities to your family as well. If you don't consider your personal health, fail to get proper sleep, or neglect your family, you are heading for massive trouble in your ability to lead, not to mention in your entire life. However, other difficulties arise when those who claim to be leaders tend to consider themselves or their personal well-being first. As the mighty corporation he ran headed south in 2008, CEO John Thain of Merrill Lynch actually hired a famous designer to redecorate his office at a cost of over $1,000,000.[5] When this became public, he paid it back out of his own pocket. Still, one has to wonder whether he was considering himself first or last when he decided to redecorate. By contrast, Ann Price, CEO of Motek, actually prides herself on having the smallest office of all her workers—and that's in good times!

If you are a leader, you have responsibilities you cannot avoid. You must take care of those you expect to follow you. You have to keep the well-being of those you lead in the forefront. You have to consider the impact of any action you take, or fail to take, on the mission. Most of all, you must do all of this before you start taking care of your own wants and needs. Yes, as a leader you have certain privileges and power that others do not. But you also have increased responsibilities. And don't forget: others will do as you do. If you consider your own well-being first—before others and before your mission—so will others. In all likelihood they probably won't follow you at all. They will be too busy looking out for themselves!

Conquest—and Care

Alexander the Great conquered the known world of his day. By the time of his death in June 323 B.C. Alexander controlled the largest area of the earth's surface ever to be conquered by a single individual (except for Genghis Khan, whose empire had lasted a shorter period). It is said that Alexander mourned the fact that there were no further worlds to conquer. Whether he actually felt this or not, it is certainly clear that a good deal of Alexander's success can be traced to his looking out for those he led, even before he looked after himself. He made certain his soldiers were well fed before every battle. Though he was weary after the Battle of Granicus (in May 334 B.C., when he entered Persia and managed to defeat a superior number of Persians under the emperor Darius), he immediately took the time to visit all of his wounded. He personally examined their wounds and asked them how they were received. He even encouraged his men to boast of their exploits. As noted by military historian John Keegan, this was "excellent psychotherapy, however wearisome for the listener."[6] Only afterward did Alexander look to his own needs and get some rest.

At the Battle of Issus in Mesopotamia, in November 333 B.C., Alexander received a sword wound in the thigh. It was not life threatening, but he was in considerable pain. As supreme commander and king, Alexander had access to the best doctors, who no doubt advised him to stay put for a couple of days. Alexander ignored their advice. Uncomfortable as he was, he again made the rounds to visit his wounded soldiers before calling it a day.[7]

Sharing the Pain

In the late 1990s, Ken Iverson was CEO of the then $4.2 billion Nucor Corporation. Nucor had enjoyed consistently high profits for thirty years in what can only be termed a declining industry: steel manufacturing. Although Nucor's seven thousand employees were the best-paid workers in the steel business, the company had the industry's lowest labor costs per ton of steel produced. When Iverson was CEO, Nucor was a Fortune 500 company with only twenty-four people working at corporate headquarters and just four layers of management from the CEO to the front-line worker. Nucor had no research and development department or corporate engineering group. Yet the company was the first major operator of "mini-mills," the first to demonstrate that mini-mills could make flat-rolled steel, the first to apply thin-stab casing, which Big Steel had determined couldn't be done, and the first to commercially produce iron carbide. Put in simple terms, Iverson had taken over a failing business and had built it into a highly successful giant. How had he done it?

The events of a few years earlier offer insight into what might be necessary during other times of significant economic challenge. When times were bad for the steel industry back in 1982, the total number of U.S. steelworkers dropped from four hundred thousand to two hundred thousand. At Nucor they had to cut production in half, but Iverson did not "downsize" anyone. How did he avoid doing what every other steel company did? Department heads took pay cuts of up to 40 percent. Iverson and other company officers cut their salaries by 60 percent and more. When even this wasn't enough, Iverson cut back workweeks from five days to four, and then to three days. This meant that on average his workers suffered a 25 percent cut in pay. "You know that had to hurt," says Iverson. "Still, as I walked through our mills and plants, I never heard one employee complain about it. Not one."[8] That's not too surprising when those workers fully understood that their leaders were taking significant cuts also.

Iverson adds, "I was in the Navy for three years and ended up as a lieutenant, junior grade. But I probably did not get my philosophies from the Navy. I was much too young (in at seventeen, out at twenty)."[9] Nevertheless, Ken Iverson clearly followed the principles of Heroic Leadership; at Nucor, he put duty before self: "I took a 75 percent pay cut from $450,000 to $110,000," he said. "It was the only right thing to do. Of course, nothing is written in stone. If we have to lay people off some day to save Nucor, we'll do it. But not before we try everything else first. We call that pain sharing. When times are good, we share the benefits, and when times are bad, leaders have to share that as well. For all of us, but leaders especially, there is a duty that comes before personal interest, and certainly before my personal interest."[10]

Summary

Heroic Leaders know they will not get others to follow them by putting their own interests ahead of the mission or those they lead. They know they must put their personal interests last. This is usually not easy to do. Still, you can heed this principle of leadership if you

- Focus on your duty.
- Put mission and people before your own needs.
- Share the pain.

CHAPTER 8

. . . .

Get Out in Front

. . . .

There is no way to lead from the rear in combat, and there is no way to lead from the rear in corporate life. You have to be "up front," where the action is. That way you can see what's going right and what's not. You can make critical decisions fast without things having to work their way up and down the chain of command for approval. You can see your people—and they can see you. With you out front there is no question in anyone's mind as to what you want done, and the fact that you are there, on the spot, lets people know just how committed you are to getting your goals accomplished. Your view from the front lets people know that you think what they are doing is important. It lets all who would follow you know that you are ready, willing, and able to share in their hardships, problems, successes, and failures in working toward every goal and completing every task. Moreover, being where the action is gives you an opportunity to set the example. Remember that to be a leader, you have to lead—and that means being out in front.

It is claimed that General George S. Patton once said, "If you want an army to fight and risk death, you've got to get up there and lead it. An army is like spaghetti. You can't push a piece of spaghetti, you've got to pull it."

. . . .

Without one leader pulling from out in front instead of pushing, the casualties in the Gulf War might have been ten times what they were. Yet it was not the actions of a senior leader like Norman Schwarzkopf or Colin Powell that made the difference but rather those of a relatively junior Naval officer. Lieutenant Commander Steve Senk was on board the USS *Tripoli* when it struck an Iraqi mine. Seawater rushed in and mixed with volatile helicopter fuel from ruptured tanks stored below decks. The air was thick with highly flammable and toxic paint thinner fumes. The flame from a single match would have ignited this mixture, causing instant detonation. The resulting inferno probably would have incinerated all aboard, including 1,375 Marines who were being transported into action.

The greatest peril was below decks where dangerous gases, both toxic and explosive, pooled. The gases had to be cleared, but no one was eager to enter that hellhole. Lieutenant Commander Senk did not order anyone into the increased danger. Instead, he got out in front, rushing below decks where he could begin the hazardous work at once. Because he went, others followed. For four hours Senk personally led the effort to decontaminate the space below decks. Though fatigued, he refused relief. Several times he almost collapsed because of the fumes. In the end, he and his men succeeded in cleansing the area. The engines were restarted, and the crippled ship reached port safely.

Recently I was contacted by Steve Senk, who had read one of my columns containing his story. He volunteered to speak at any seminar I gave in the San Diego area, where he lives. Senk is truly a great leader and a practitioner of Heroic Leadership. If business leaders could motivate their employees to perform at a small fraction of the dedication of Commander Senk and his sailors, what could their organizations not accomplish? I believe business leaders can inspire such motivation if they get out in front. Employees don't follow leaders who spend all their time behind desks. They follow leaders who get out where they can see and be seen, who set the example. These take-charge leaders aren't afraid to mix with the people actually doing the work.

Leading in Combat

Confederate general Robert E. Lee exposed himself so frequently in the front lines of battle that his soldiers were terrified he might be killed. They promised him victory if he would just go to a more protected area. They would take up the cry, "General Lee to the rear! General Lee to the rear!" Federal general Ulysses S. Grant was in the company of his soldiers as much as his generals. One wrote home that General Grant was so much exposed to enemy fire that soldiers were ashamed to do less or be thought a coward.

But don't get the idea that successful generals got out in front only during the nineteenth century. Major General Maurice Rose commanded the Third Armor Division in Europe during World War II. Many knew the Third Armor Division in those days because it had been the first division to capture a German town. General Rose was killed in action out in front while leading his men in an attack on March 30, 1945. In the Philippines, during the same war, Douglas MacArthur was frequently up front with his troops in combat. As reported by one veteran newsman, he shocked one private who had spotted him. "General MacArthur," he exclaimed, "we killed a sniper not ten minutes ago, right over there." "Good," responded MacArthur, "that's what to do with them." In the first B-52 raid in Vietnam, two generals were killed when the airplane in which they were flying collided with another. In Desert Storm, in Panama, in all wars, successful commanders try not to take what they consider to be unnecessary risks. However, when risks are necessary, senior leaders get right out front where the action is.

When on active duty, Brigadier General Harry "Heinie" Aderholt was the dean of Air Force Air Commando leaders. He led in combat in World War II and Korea, and had nine years' combat experience during the Vietnam War, where he saw action in Vietnam, Laos, and Cambodia. General Aderholt said, "There's no secret about leadership. You've got to know your people, live with them, and be seen always out front."[1]

Out Front with the Piranhas

As president of Inland Laboratories in Austin, Texas, Dr. Mark Chandler built a $100 million company with a different kind of product. Inland sells toxins, viruses, and other biochemical products to medical researchers. One time Inland needed two rare plants to refine into a cancer medicine. These plants grew only in a Brazilian rainforest hundreds of miles from civilization. Chandler couldn't buy them anywhere. Someone had to go into the jungle and harvest the plants. Perhaps Chandler could have sent employees to find this rare foliage. However, their job descriptions did not include facing piranhas, deadly snakes, and headhunters. He knew this was one trip no one else could lead.

Dr. Mark Chandler got out in front. He personally organized and led an eight-day expedition up the Amazon. The going was not easy: several days into the journey he thought he was going to die. Burning up with fever and racked by diarrhea, he plunged into the river to cool off, forgetting about piranhas and poisonous snakes. He was so sick, he just didn't care. Two days later the fever broke; shortly after, with the help of native guides, he got his plants. David Nance, president of Intron Therapeutics and a customer for more than ten years, says, "Mark is equally comfortable in a loincloth, lab coat, or a three-piece suit." Customers and employees know that Chandler can be counted on to be out in front where the action is.[2] Chandler went on to found other successful corporations and to serve as their CEO.[3]

General Wallace "Wally" Nutting retired from the Army as a four-star general and the commander in chief of Southern Command, a major regional command. General Nutting states that successful combat leaders set the example, that they just about always lead from the front. Moreover, they should be willing to do not only everything they ask of their followers, but more. "Once I entered a defensive minefield at night with a French sergeant to remove an injured Korean woman—a necessary act at the time, but not one I felt I should ask one of my platoons to accomplish," he recalls.[4]

Why You Must Get Out in Front

Do you remember the children's game "Follow the Leader"? Followers try to do everything the leader does. They rarely hesitate, because they see the leader do it first. Indeed, no less a Heroic Leader than Gideon is quoted in the Bible saying, "As I do, so shall you do."

Some leaders feel they must maintain total detachment. They believe they must coolly and carefully analyze the facts and make a decision without being influenced by outside complications. From their viewpoint this process must occur away from the action to avoid the noise, pressures of time, and other problems that detract from their ability to think calmly and clearly.

There is a place for contemplative thinking and measured analysis in leadership. But many leaders have their priorities all wrong. The first priority is that the leader must get out where the action is, where those who are doing the actual work are making things happen. Leaders cannot lead from behind a desk in an air-conditioned office. Military historian John Keegan, who wrote the classic treatise on the essence of military leadership, *The Mask of Command*, concludes, "The first and greatest imperative of command is to be present in person."[5]

Women in Battle and in Boardrooms

According to the Bible, Deborah was a judge of Israel. Among her duties was military advisement. Called to advise the Hebrew general Barak in the Israelites' war against the Canaanites of

Jabon, Deborah suggested that Barak recruit ten thousand troops and invade Jabon. According to Judges 4:8–9, Barak was not entirely convinced. "If thou wilt go with me, then I will go; but if thou will not go with me, then I will not go." Deborah did go, and her presence up front inspired the Israelites to victory. She received full credit: "The people were oppressed in Israel, until you arose, Deborah, as the mother of Israel," the Holy Scriptures say.

There are modern Deborahs in the boardroom as well as the battlefield, women who get out in front today. Beth Pritchard was the chief executive of the nation's leading bath-shop chain, Bath & Body Works. Pritchard got out in front and demonstrated a special power, too. In addition to her corporate duties and responsibilities, she spent two days a month working "in the trenches" in a Bath & Body Works boutique. Pritchard didn't sit around observing or spend all her time handing out advice to employees. She saw and was seen; she taught and she learned. She helped set up displays, stock shelves, and arrange gift baskets, "though I'm not really good on the cash register," she claims. Whether she was good on the cash register seems not to have mattered. Her cash registers were full. The power of getting out in front paid off. When Pritchard took over Bath & Body Works in 1991, it had 95 stores and sales of $20 million. Five years later, the number of stores had increased to a whopping 750, and sales hit $753 million.[6] Maybe this is why she went on to a number of senior management positions in other top companies.[7]

Two Generals Set the Example

Napoleon Bonaparte advised commanders to always march toward the sounds of the guns. This is good advice for commanders in uniform or executives in mufti. It was his way of saying, "Go where the action is." Well-known management author Tom Peters, who himself served as an officer in the Navy, recommends going where the action is as a management process and calls it "management by wandering about."

Two four-star generals showed all of us how this is done. When the C-17 air transport aircraft was accepted by the Air Force, General Ronald Fogleman enthusiastically received it. General Fogleman, who later became Air Force chief of staff, from 1995 until 1997, wore two hats at the time. He was commander of Air Mobility Command (AMC) at Scott Air Force Base, near Belleville, Illinois. AMC would operate the C-17. In addition, he was commander in chief of U.S. Transportation Command, which is responsible for strategic logistical support by all means, land, sea, and air, around the world.

The C-17 represented a giant leap forward in air transport. It could fly farther and faster and carry more weight than other Air Force strategic transports. Moreover, it could get into unimproved fields where other military jet transports like the C-141 or C-5 could not. Like the C-141 it was capable of carrying and dropping a full load of army paratroops.

Some Army officers involved in airborne operations were not happy, however. ("Airborne operations" is what the military calls operations involving parachutists.) A rumor was circulating that a spoiler extended to help reduce airspeed of the C-17 during airdrops would pose a hazard to paratroopers as they exited the aircraft. This had certainly been tested previously, and it had worked. "But," said these officers, "that doesn't mean there still isn't a potential problem." The aircraft was dangerous for paratroopers, they claimed, and there was talk that some troops might even refuse to jump from a C-17 because of the risk of striking the spoiler.

Around this time, an unannounced airplane landed at Edwards Air Force Base in California, where the C-17 was undergoing its final tests. Two generals got out of the plane. One was Lieutenant General Henry H. Shelton, a Master Parachutist with hundreds of jumps. He probably had more jumps than any other general in the armed services. In 1997 President Clinton appointed him to be chairman of the Joint Chiefs of Staff, after commanding the U.S. Special Operations Command. In those days, Shelton was commander of the Army's 18th Airborne Corps at Ft. Bragg, North Carolina. His organization included the 82nd Airborne Division, which would be the prime user of the C-17 as a jump vehicle. The other general was Ron Fogleman. He normally flew airplanes rather than jumping out of them, but he was a rated parachutist. He had graduated from the Army's Parachute School at Fort Benning, Georgia, thirty years earlier and had made his required five jumps to earn his parachute wings, later going back to parachute school to get requalified. Both generals suited up in parachutes and received instruction on the peculiarities of jumping out of a C-17. They then took off in a C-17 and jumped out of it. Generals Shelton and Fogleman deemed the C-17 acceptable as an air drop vehicle, which squelched the rumors about the C-17 being unsafe for jumpers.

Others Want to See You Do It First

Jodie Glore was president and chief operating officer of Rockwell Automation, a $4.5 billion company located in Milwaukee, Wisconsin, when I spoke with him about ten years ago. Later he went on to become CEO of Iomega. In 2007 he received an award for outstanding leadership from his alma mater, West Point.[8] During the Vietnam War, Glore had been a frontline infantry company commander in the U.S. Army's 101st Airborne Division. Early during his tour of duty, his unit got in a fierce firefight with the enemy. One of his men who was out toward the front stood up and was instantly shot in the shoulder. Captain Glore ordered one of his men to crawl forward and bring the wounded man to back to cover. No one moved. Glore looked around and instantly realized that his men were waiting to see what he would do. Without hesitation, he handed his M-16 to a noncommissioned officer crouching nearby, and crawled out to retrieve the wounded man himself.

"From then on," states Glore, "they knew I was for real. When I gave an order, they obeyed it instantly, because they knew that I was ready to do it myself. This is a lesson that has served me as well in my civilian career as it has in combat."[9]

How can business leaders set the example?

Becoming an Up-Front Leader

When Julie Culwell became manager of editorial services at the Coca-Cola Company, she first tried distancing herself from her subordinates. "I'd read a lot of management books that warned me not to get personally involved with my team," she says. But things weren't working out, so she threw these books away and became an up-front leader.

"We helped pull each other through professional and personal crises. We spent time together after hours. And what happened was, the more I nurtured them, the more they produced. In fact, they became passionate about their work—putting in long hours at the office and taking projects home with them. Nobody ever missed a deadline, and the feedback we got from our clients was consistently outstanding."[10]

I'm not talking here about being a good guy and clapping people on the back, but about being unafraid to be with your people, looking them in the eye, helping them when you can, and listening to what they say. It is not important that they like you and think of you as a "good guy." What matters is that they respect you and think of you as a human being willing to share their victories and defeats.

The Disk Drive King

Alan F. Shugart was founder and CEO of Seagate Technology, the top disk drive maker at the time of this story. You could probably have called him the Disk Drive King. Seagate Technology (based in Scotts Valley, California) owned 33 percent of a $25 billion industry. Al Shugart was known to be gruff and hard driving. His technical ability was not minuscule. This was the man who had developed the first disk drive for a computer at IBM way back in 1961. Yet despite his considerable technical ability, those who worked with him and for him credit his success to his leadership. When Shugart left IBM for the Memorex Corporation in 1969, he took two hundred IBM engineers with him. These were the golden days of IBM, when "Big Blue" was the place to be for prestige, security, and monetary rewards. James N. Porter, a market analyst who worked at Memorex then, recalls, "All he had to do was raise the flag to get people to work with him."[11]

Shugart demanded hard work, and he was not a leader that avoided difficult decisions. He demoted former vice president Robert Martell, who could easily have become president of another company. Instead, Shugart offered him a lower-ranking job and convinced him to take it. Martell went to Europe to take charge of Seagate's new European subsidiary. Within a year, he had tripled sales and was back home in a better position. Martell said, "I'd do almost anything Al asked me to do."

What was Shugart's secret? One of his vice presidents, Stephen J. Luczo, says, "He's the most up-front guy I've ever worked with."[12] After-hours, Shugart used to hold impromptu staff meetings at local bars. Since he showed up everywhere wearing short sleeves and never wore a tie, he was always ready for such informal meetings. The most popular location at one time was a tavern called Malone's. Employees called it "Building 13," a reference to Seagate's twelve-building complex. Shugart was successful because he had mastered the art of getting out in front and staying there twenty-four hours a day. At his death in 2006 it was said of him that his career defined the industry.[13]

Summary

When the USS *Tripoli* struck a mine, Commander Senk didn't sit at his desk and ponder the decontamination job below decks. In the battlefield or the boardroom, Heroic Leaders know that if you want people to follow you, you must lead from the front. To do this,

- Go where the action is.
- Set the example.
- Be willing to do anything you ask your people to do.
- Take charge.
- Be an up-front leader.

PART TWO

The Eight Basic Influence Tools

In battle, in business, and in the rest of our lives, we lead others by influencing them. Sometimes this influence just seems to happen, but even experienced leaders can frequently lead better by consciously selecting and applying tactics from this list of eight tools examined in turn in the next chapters:

- Direction
- Indirection
- Redirection
- Deflection
- Enlistment
- Persuasion
- Negotiation
- Involvement

Learning the proper use of these tools will equip you with the arsenal to make you a powerful and Heroic Leader.

CHAPTER 9

• •

Direction

• •

Sometimes simply giving orders with no discussion is your best choice. To employ this tool—direction—successfully, you must have more power in the situation than those you intend to lead. If you try to lead this way without having some kind of authority, not only will you probably fail, but you may damage the relationship permanently.

The first situation in which you may want to use direction is when there is too little time for the other influence tools. What you need accomplished needs to be done now, with no time for discussion. In combat, the leader must frequently be authoritarian and rely heavily on direction for influence. There is no time for dilly-dallying when a slight delay can cause a major defeat or cost lives.

The second situation is when the needed action, though perhaps good for the organization, is less desirable for individuals; for example, it may bring about unwanted change in the old culture or in the way things have been done. Not infrequently, the need for direction is a combination of these two situations. While you can try to use the other influence tools first, eventually the best approach may come down to using direction. How you give direction can make all the difference. Sometimes you have to be very creative.

Direction on the Ground

In 1993 my son Barak graduated from Ranger School in the Army. In Ranger School different battlefield missions requiring extended time in the field are assigned. Each mission lasts about eight weeks and falls into four phases involving urban, jungle, desert, and mountain commando warfare. An instructor accompanies each team of Ranger trainees. He assigns leadership roles on a rotating basis and grades the students on their performance. While in the field, Ranger trainees get little food and are sleep-deprived. The levels of physical exertion, stress, and real danger are all significant. The elimination rate is usually 60 percent or higher for the course.

In the mountain (cold weather) phase, my son's team included a number of his West Point classmates. After several days in the field one of his classmates, who was leading the group, observed that another Ranger student, also a West Pointer, seemed to be faltering and actually fell in the snow. The student team leader went to the fallen student, yanked him roughly to his feet, and spoke to him in a threatening manner. My son was standing next to the instructor; neither of them heard what the student leader said. The instructor beckoned the student leader over. "What did you say to that guy?" he asked. "I said that if he didn't get his act together I was going to beat the living shit out of him," answered the team leader. The instructor nodded and said, "That's the way to do it."

Barak knew that I don't normally recommend this very physical style of leadership, and he wanted to know what I thought. I told him that I agreed with the instructor. Under these circumstances—with everyone tired, hungry, and greatly stressed—the other leadership influence tools were unlikely to be effective, especially since both the student leader and the trainee who fell were West Point classmates and presumably knew each other before entering Ranger training.

According to my son, this approach did work, and the faltering trainee completed the mission without further incident. I told my son that while he would be ill advised to use this influence tool on a routine basis, it was a valid tool he could pull from his leadership bag of tricks when needed and when he had the authority to pull it off. In this instance the selection of the direction tactic was exactly right.

I have also heard of this tool being used in a similar physical fashion within a civilian setting by a first-line supervisor. An individual had been consistently avoiding work and bullying other members of the group to do his work for him. The correction worked. Of course, using direction in such a physical manner can be extremely risky. If you try it, you really have to know what you are doing, lest you be charged with assault, sued, or fired—or all three. It all depends on the many factors in the situation and in the environment. Extreme application of the direction tool, then, is almost always not a good idea. Usually, just issuing orders, if the leader has the authority, is enough. And that is the usual application of the direction tool.

Nonverbal Orders

On November 14, 2004, Colonel James Coffman was senior adviser with the First Iraqi Special Police Commando Brigade in Mosul, Iraq, when it came under a surprise attack by a large force of insurgents. Coffman was seriously wounded, and all but one of the Iraqi officers in the brigade were killed. Having no interpreter, Coffman led this brigade while under attack for four hours by going from man to man giving orders. Yet none of these men spoke English, and Coffman spoke no Arabic.

Coffman won this battle solely by looking each man in the eyes and telling him what to do while using hand and arm signals.[1] Even with verbal means, using direction as an influence tool can be a tough job. For Colonel Coffman, not speaking the language, it was a tougher challenge still. But he pulled it off.

Giving Up a Holiday

Grace Pastiak worked for Tellabs in Lisle, Illinois. Tellabs designs, makes, and markets expensive telecommunications products. When she was director of manufacturing, her department won a major contract. The only problem was that it was the holiday season, and the job had to be completed by the end of the year.

Grace always took pride in her group's ability to take on any job and complete it successfully. So did her group. But now she faced a dilemma. Accepting this job would mean time away from families during the Christmas holidays. The contract was very important; she did not want to turn it down. Grace knew that she needed the full support of her workers. But how could she attempt to get that without arousing resentment? She knew that under the circumstances she needed to use some form of the direction tool. So Grace did something she had never done before. She called her employees together and explained all the facts face-to-face. She told them that the job had to be completed by the end of the year. She told them the job was so important that they *were* going to take the contract. To this she was committed. She also told them that it would involve time away from home at Christmas and New Year. They would be able to attend religious services, but that was about it.

This was certainly giving direction, but how could she gain their support? Grace was committed to the project and willing to do whatever it took. However, because of the extent of the sacrifice necessary, the employees would help make the decision. There were alternatives, and she offered several. They could contract to do only half of the order before the deadline. They could bring part-time labor in. Or they could subcontract some of the production to other companies. She told them again that she wanted to take the whole contract and accept the deadline as they had always done, but it was their choice. Grace made direction more acceptable by giving her workers a choice.

Giving her workers a choice on how to do the job also proved that this was not a regular job order, and that it was extremely important. The workers voted to take the full contract and not to bring in part-time workers or subcontract any of the work. The contract was completed during the holiday season without difficulty. Is it any wonder that subordinates and superiors alike call Pastiak "Amazing Grace"?[2]

Overuse of Direction

Once you begin using direction as an influence tool routinely, it becomes habit. It's so easy to use—and overuse. You don't have to think about those you lead at all. You simply issue an order. General Bernard Rodgers, who spent more than twelve years as a four-star general and senior Army commander once jokingly said that his biggest shock after retirement was when he got in the backseat of his car and waited for the car to pull out. In the Army, his driver didn't need a verbal order. The fact that Rodgers was sitting there was enough; the driver knew where to go. But the car didn't move. For the first time in twelve years General Rodgers had no driver. He was sitting in the car by himself.

Routinely using direction can have unwanted results. You may discover that you no longer get input from those you lead. "Fine," say your followers. "If that so-and-so wants us to do this and everything gets screwed up, it's not our fault." Mistakes you make that others might have caught are allowed to go uncorrected. Soon your organization is brought to a standstill. Yet everyone goes about following your orders to the letter. And that's just the trouble.

Erroneous Assumptions

When you use the direction tactic, you've got to make sure it's employed in the right way. Many just give orders and assume they are understood. They may not be. Back in 1941, while the nation was tooling up for World War II, aircraft companies were hiring engineers as fast as they graduated. Unfortunately, some of the managers in these organizations had not been given proper training in leadership. One engineering supervisor in the Boeing Aircraft Company in Seattle was assigned five recently graduated engineers. On their first day of work, he dealt out jobs one after the other in an automatic fashion. He didn't explain them, nor did he encourage questions or ask if those on the receiving end understood the job he wanted done. Handing one new engineer a set of master aluminum "blueprints" for the B-17 engine, he directed, "I want these cleaned so there isn't a spot on them. And I want them finished by this afternoon. Now, go. Hop to it!"

These "blueprint" masters were aluminum engravings containing the manufacturing and assembly specifications for the engine. An engraving was the master used to print the paper version, which was in turn used on the production line. The aluminum blueprints had picked up ink and grease from use. What was wanted was to clean the ink and grease from these valuable masters. They were valued at about $10,000 each (worth many times that in today's dollars). The supervisor had said that he wanted them cleaned so that "there wasn't a spot on them." Not understanding this order, the raw engineer got some Brillo pads and with considerable effort polished the metal until it gleamed—and scrubbed off the important engravings. He was fired when he presented the engravings proudly to the supervisor at the end of the day.

They fired the wrong man. The engineering supervisor who gave the order to an inexperienced engineer should have been the one to go. When you use direction, be particularly careful not to make assumptions about the instructions you give. They could cause a disaster.

Misplaced Direction

Another reason that you don't want to use the direction tactic under any or all conditions is that, even if it works, it might not serve your own best interests. I knew a young lieutenant who got so much into giving direction that he used it not only in leading his subordinates but with his colleagues and superiors as well. He confused leadership with dominating others. For a while he was successful. He was so bold in giving his direction, and frequently right, that everyone just did what he wanted. He was discharged after receiving several poor officer's effectiveness reports. What was his offense? The report didn't use these words, but it boiled down to one fact. He used a perfectly good influence tool under inappropriate conditions and in an inappropriate manner. You can certainly lead your associates and even your boss, but rarely by giving orders.

Summary

The leader should recognize that direction is one of many influence tools. It is not a substitute for other leadership tools. The Heroic Leader must consider the following:

- Direction has its uses, but don't invoke it in any or every instance; it may not be in your best interest or the organization's.

- Direction can be combined with other tools or options which allow giving choice to subordinates.

- This is the right tool when time is limited, when you have the authority, or when what needs to be done is particularly difficult or may be more in the organization's interest than that of the individuals who will need to take the requested action.

CHAPTER 10

● ●

Indirection

● ●

Indirection is frequently used when your authority in the situation is limited and those you want to lead may resist direction. However, it can also be used with great effectiveness when you have the authority to give direct orders, and others know it. In other words, your influence is exerted without direct instructions to better attain a tactical goal.

Influence for Leading Up

Children—whose lives are the classic case of influence in a low-power situation—use the indirection tool frequently. If you have children, you know you need to watch out when they begin to act particularly nice, offer to do extra work, or tell you how well you look. You are about to be led by the indirection influence tactic. As a parent, the formal power is yours. But you are being led by the informal power of charm. Do you know where you are being led? You may not, but you soon will. Chances are your son wants to borrow the car, or your daughter wants to go out on a date in the middle of the week.

In my son's case, what he wanted was a computer. When my second son, Nimrod (named for the Bible's first hunter, and for my squadron in Vietnam), was about twelve, he became very interested in computers. Neither my wife nor I owned one at the time, and they were expensive. Even a used Apple, with laughable memory compared to today's systems, cost a lot of money. Nimrod talked about computers all the time. He got books and magazines and read about computers. He took a special course on computers given at summer school for older students. He wanted a computer—badly. Nimrod started saving his money. But there isn't a lot twelve-year-olds can do to earn money. Even the paper routes of my youth, which were my way to cash, are generally no longer available. Working every day after school, he started doing odd jobs going door to door. My wife and I calculated that at the rate he was going, it would take years for him to come up with the money. But he kept at it for several months, and continued eating, living, and breathing computers.

"Maybe we should just buy him one," suggested my wife. "No way," said I. "They cost too much money. He'll earn enough eventually." Yeah, right.

One day, I walked into his room to find it spotlessly clean. Moreover, not only was everything in order, but several tables had been set against the wall with nothing on them. A straight back chair was placed before the center table. "What's this?" I inquired. Big mistake, that question. "It's for my computer," Nimrod answered. I turned around and left the room immediately. That afternoon my wife and I got a "Recycler" newspaper, which listed used items for sale. That evening, Nimrod had his computer. Note that he had never asked for one. Nimrod had led us where he wanted using the indirection tactic.

If our kids did this all the time, it probably wouldn't work. Still, it's amazing how often we do allow our children to lead us this way even though we may know what's happening. And so Johnny gets to use the car, and even though we intended to encourage her to stay home and study, Sarah gets to go out Wednesday night.

And Influence for Leading Down

At the close of the Revolutionary War the Continental Army had not yet disbanded, and Congress was slow in authorizing back pay. The righting of various other wrongs had been frequently promised by the Continental Congress but never fulfilled. The Continental Army officers knew that George Washington would never go along with seizing power from the civilian authority, no matter how just the cause. They asked him anyway. They wanted to march on Congress and give Washington the title of "Dictator." This was wrong. It was treason, and he told them so, only they wouldn't listen. Moreover, he was no longer their official commander and so had no formal power over them.

The officers had a meeting to organize what amounted to a rebellion. Washington went. He hoped to dissuade them, and they actually let him speak. Washington spoke to the officers for more than an hour. Remember, these weren't mercenaries or shirkers. Among them were many of the heroes of the revolution, men like Alexander Hamilton, John Knox, and "Light Horse" Harry Lee, who all listened to Washington. Washington talked about why they had fought, what would happen should they rebel, and what Congress was trying to do. It was to no avail. Too many times before had they received promises from Congress only to see them broken. The officers were determined to take the law into their own hands!

Finally, Washington reached into his cloak and pulled out a pair of spectacles. No one had ever seen Washington with spectacles before. In the thinking of the day, it was the kind of physical weakness that commanders didn't admit to. As he slowly put the glasses to his face, he said his final words to his former officers. "Gentlemen, I have grown old in your service and now I am growing blind." There wasn't a dry eye in the house. Washington turned and left. At first there was only silence. Then somebody said, "Oh, what the heck. Maybe George is right. Let's give Congress one more chance." The rebellion, of course, never took place.

Washington's officers didn't know that he had worn spectacles for years. Even his closest aides hadn't known. Washington judged that the loss of his vanity and the risk of his prestige in opposing this treason was a worthwhile price to pay for an America that would be free from a military dictatorship. Using indirection as an influence tool, he got what he wanted after other influence tools had failed.

How Quality Came to Japan

"The Father of Modern Management," Peter Drucker, spent years working and consulting with Japanese companies. Commenting on "Theory Z" back when it was thought this was the end-all solution to managing American companies, Drucker maintained that it wasn't so much "quality circles" or some other unique technique used in Japan that had changed the quality of Japanese goods. Rather, Deming, Juran, and others had made Japanese leaders *aware* of a problem with quality. After that, Japanese business leaders knew what had to be done and took the necessary actions to focus on quality. This redirected the emphasis to a subject which had previously been ignored or thought unimportant in their companies. "Quality circles" and other techniques taught by Deming and Juran supported that effort, but the entire quality movement came about through indirection!

Getting Things Done in Government

One of my most amazing West Point classmates is Frederic V. Malek. Fred saw combat in Vietnam in 1961 as a regular infantry lieutenant attached to the First Special Forces Group advising Vietnamese Ranger companies.[1] After leaving the Army, he put himself through Harvard Business School selling encyclopedias. While still a young man, he rescued a failing company in South Carolina and became a multimillionaire by the age of thirty. Recruited by the Nixon White House, he served as deputy undersecretary of the Department of Health, Education and Welfare, special assistant to the president, and finally deputy director of the Office of Management and Budget (OMB). Then he left government and joined the Marriott Corporation, becoming president of the Marriott Hotels, president of Northwest Airlines, and chairman of Thayer/ Hidden Creek, a private equity firm specializing in lower-middle-market leveraged buyouts. Along the way, he helped the elder President Bush, serving in senior positions in both of his campaigns. Few have accomplished so much or made so many contributions in so many fields.[2]

Back in 1973, though, Fred had a problem. Appointed to the important position of deputy director of OMB, he was frustrated. He couldn't get things done very quickly because of layers of career bureaucrats who occupied the key positions. Early on he spotted a White House Fellow, an army major, who seemed to know what he was doing. His name was Colin Powell. Fred made Powell his executive assistant. I'll let General Powell pick up the story: "Fred went about gaining control of the government in a way that opened the eyes of this fledgling student of power. . . . Fred started planting his own people in the key 'assistant secretary for administration' slots in major federal agencies. Let the cabinet officials make the speeches, cut the ribbons, and appear on *Meet the Press*. Anonymous assistant secretaries, loyal to Malek, would run operations day to day, and to the Nixon administration's liking. . . . I learned much in Professor Malek's graduate seminar."[3]

Bureaucrats already occupied many positions in OMB, however, and the budget couldn't be increased to create more positions for the young Harvard, Stanford, and Wharton graduates Fred wanted to bring in. So he applied the influence tool of indirection in a very creative way. Continues Powell, "Thereafter, I started phoning agency officials, explaining that I was calling on behalf of Mr. Malek with good news. Their power was about to be broadened. A function currently being handled by OMB was going to be transferred to their agency . . . music to any bureaucrat's ear."[4] Then Powell would go on to explain that the agency would get the function and the bodies, but not the position titles and funding. "'We don't have jobs for them. We haven't budgeted funds for them.' 'Mr. Assistant Secretary,' I would say, 'Fred Malek has every confidence that between attrition and some imagination on your part, you will work something out.' Soon the unwanted OMB bureaucrats were gone, their offices and titles freed up, and Malek's young bloods moved in. Out of that experience emerged one of my rules: you don't know what you can get away with until you try."[5]

Donald Trump and Indirection

Donald Trump has become well known for *The Apprentice* on television, especially at the conclusion of a session "in the boardroom" when he leans forward, gestures dramatically, and tells one of the competitors, "You're fired." That's direction with a capital D. Yet Trump is a strong believer in the use of indirection as an influence tool. He tells the story of how the manager of the Grand Hyatt was successful in leading him with indirection after a predecessor had failed and was discharged.

Trump had built the Grand Hyatt and still owned a 50 percent interest. The former manager couldn't stand the interference of Trump and his wife, so he complained to the head of the Hyatt Hotels. This got the manager himself replaced. His replacement was more skilled at leadership and using the influence tools. According to Trump, "The new manager did something brilliant. He began to bombard us with trivia. He'd call up several times a week, and he'd say, 'Donald, we want your approval to change the wallpaper on the fourteenth floor' or 'We want to introduce a new menu in one of the restaurants' or 'We are thinking of switching to a new laundry service.' They'd also invite us to all of their management meetings. The guy went so far out of his way to solicit our opinions and involve us in the hotel that finally I said, 'Leave me alone; do whatever you want, just don't bother me.' What he did was the perfect ploy, because he got what he wanted not by fighting but by being positive and friendly and solicitous."[6] I said earlier that we must sometimes use Heroic Leadership to lead people at our level, or even our bosses. That was what my son did in gaining his computer, and that's what Trump's hotel manager did. It is what you can do as well.

Writer James Clavell pointed out a similar incident in his book *Tai-Pan*. Clavell had been a professional soldier; he had served in combat during World War II and was at the rank of captain when a motorcycle accident ended his military career.[7] *Tai-Pan* is about the English founder and head of a great British Trading Company in nineteenth century China. The head of the company was known as the "Tai-Pan." At the end of the book, the Tai-Pan is killed in a typhoon. His eighteen-year-old son, with little experience or training, is suddenly thrust into major responsibilities as the company's head. At first he is shocked into silence. He doesn't know what to say or do. His subordinates are standing around waiting for him to take charge and give first orders. There is a pause as none of the new Tai-Pan's senior managers say a word. Suddenly, the former Tai-Pan's right-hand man, who is Chinese, turns to the new head of the firm and in a pleading voice asks, "Tai-Pan, Tai-Pan, what should we do?" This man had years of experience and could have instantly given the orders that needed to be given. His deferring to the eighteen-year-old shocked the young man into the realization that he was now in charge; ready or not, he had to take over and assert his authority—which he did. This is a perfect example of leading a superior and, in doing so, using indirection.

Indirection in the Navy

Mike Abrashoff's amazing success in making the ship which he captained, the USS *Benfold*, the best in the Pacific Fleet resulted in several best-selling books. A strong element in Abrashoff's leadership was his use of indirection as an influence tool.

For example, he began writing letters to parents praising their sons when they did something worthy. On one occasion he wrote to both parents, who had recently divorced. Two weeks later the young sailor reported to Abrashoff with tears streaming down his face. "What's wrong?" Abrashoff asked. The sailor answered, "'I just got a call from my father, who all my life told me I'm a failure. This time, he said he'd just read your letter, and he wanted to congratulate me and say how proud he was of me. It's the first time in my entire life he's actually encouraged me. Captain, I can't thank you enough.' My own tear ducts held, but I was very moved."[8] Is it any wonder that the sailors on the USS *Benfold* wanted to perform at the highest levels? Yet what Captain Abrashoff did was to ask for this level of performance indirectly.

Summary

- Indirection is almost the exact opposite of the direction tool. You actually get what you want by *not* giving orders, and sometimes by not even mentioning your objective.

- Indirection works well in many situations because it shifts the focus and control of the desired action from the leader to those being led.

- Indirection can work wonders in leading others—such as peers and superiors—over whom you have limited authority, but it can also work well, and even better than the direction tool, when you do have the authority.

- To use the indirection tool, first decide what you want done, then take an action which will help those you lead understand your objective without your having to declare it.

CHAPTER 11

• •

Redirection

• •

I once heard a story about a woman who was poised a hundred feet above the water outside the safety bar of a bridge, threatening to commit suicide. A policeman a few feet away talked to the woman and tried to persuade her to climb off her perch. He first tried to convince her that regardless of her problems, her life was worth living. That didn't work. He tried to order her down. That didn't work either. He tried negotiation and all the other techniques taught by law enforcement and psychologists in suicide situations. Nothing worked. The woman remained in place, ready to jump. Finally, in desperation, the police officer shouted, "Lady, you can jump if you want, but I sure wouldn't want to jump into that dirty water. It's full of sewage and garbage, and smells awful." She hesitated, and after a few minutes' consideration moved back to a point where the police officer was able to pull her to safety. The police officer had used redirection as an influence tool in his successful rescue.

Using Redirection

The leader using redirection may not want to reveal the real reason for the desired action. The followers need redirection to avoid a negative impact of one kind or another. Let's say there are two organizations whose offices are located right next to each other. The members of these organizations are constantly bickering. The fact that they are located so close to one another allows more opportunity for hostile contact. Having their offices moved apart physically separates the two staffs. Does the memo announcing the move state that they are being relocated because of their bickering? Of course not. The stated reason is probably "efficiency" or "better space utilization."

Redirection is sometimes used when firing senior managers. Senior executives are frequently not officially fired. Rather, they are removed from their positions and given new assignments. We say that they are "kicked upstairs." This is a perfectly legitimate tactic with many advantages. We preserve the feelings of the fired executive as best we can. We show others that people are important to us. We don't just curtly dismiss people who have made contributions to our organization, even if we must relieve them of their responsibilities. What's more, an individual now unsuitable for one job may do superior work in a different position. Of course, managers who have committed legal, moral, or ethical violations might be fired both to remove them and to send the message that such behavior is unacceptable, but this is something else.

Leaders in meetings frequently use the redirection tool, and in a variety of ways. If two team members are locked in a contentious argument, the leader may defer a decision to later in the meeting—or even a later meeting—as an excuse using time or the need to discuss other aspects before the issue can be finalized. This action redirects the discussion to break the focus on the argument to a time when tempers will have cooled and a more reasoned decision can be made.

Redirection in a Crisis

The redirection tool can be used at any time to refocus others on an alternative objective. On August 7, 1998, members of what was then a new terrorist group known as al Qaeda bombed the

U.S. embassies in Nairobi, Kenya, and Dar es Salaam in Tanzania. The terrorists picked the Nairobi embassy partly because a woman, Prudence Bushnell, was ambassador to Kenya. They reasoned that a woman's death would gain even greater notoriety for their act. Bushnell survived, however, and it was she who held things together in the aftermath of the bombing. She did it using a form of redirection. Although the embassy was unsafe for occupancy, she refused to shut it down. She did move herself and her staff to nearby temporary quarters so they could continue their work, but morale was low with the frustration that little could be done immediately to get back at the terrorists or bring them to justice. So Bushnell had a quotation hung in large letters where all would see it every day. It read, "Courage doesn't always roar. Sometimes courage is the quiet voice at the end of the day saying, 'I will try again tomorrow.'"

That single quote reminded everyone that just because immediate action against the terrorists was not possible, it did not mean the terrorists would succeed in shutting down the American embassy or stopping its work. Years later, as dean of the leadership and management school at the Foreign Service Institute, Bushnell kept the quote on display in her office. She taught senior officials that even when things look hopeless, a focus on the future and eventual success was needed and that this was always possible to promote.[1]

General Grant and Redirection

Ulysses S. Grant was the man Lincoln finally found to defeat Confederate general Robert E. Lee, who had been so successful. To beat Lee, Grant used the tactic of redirection to influence his men. At Grant's first battle as the head of the Army of the Potomac, Lee won the day and Union forces retreated. In the past, after a defeat, the Army of the Potomac had always retreated in the direction of Washington, the Federal capital. This time, as they retreated out of the wilderness, the Federal columns got only as far as the Chancellorsville House crossroad. There they encountered a heavyset, bearded general wearing a private's uniform and smoking a cigar. He was sitting on horseback. The unusual-looking general might not have been recognized by most of his soldiers, but he was in fact their commander, General Grant. As the head of each regiment came abreast of where Grant sat on horseback, the general took the cigar from his mouth and pointed it toward the right fork in the road. That's where they went, still thinking they were in retreat. But the right fork led straight back into battle, this time against Lee's flank.[2]

Redirection in an Impossible Situation

Redirection may mean thinking about and doing things in a way you have not considered previously. It can mean taking creative risks and doing the unthinkable. More than a hundred and fifty years ago a certain scholarly professor, finding his situation impossible, did the unthinkable and helped hard-bitten veterans do the impossible. He did this by using the redirection tool. This professor was named for the biblical warrior Joshua. His middle name was also that of a warrior's: Lawrence. His father had named him for Commodore Lawrence, hero of the War of 1812. Lawrence was famous for uttering the words, "Don't give up the ship." The professor's last name was Chamberlain.

Professor Chamberlain had been teaching at Bowdoin College in Maine when Fort Sumter was fired on in 1861. He believed strongly in the Union cause and resolved to fight for it. He asked for a leave of absence in order to enlist in the Union Army. His request was not approved. Professor Chamberlain, though only in his twenties, held one of the most important and prestigious chairs at the college, "Professor of Rhetoric and Oratory." The college didn't want him to "waste his time" with nonacademic pursuits in a war.

Professor Chamberlain then asked for sabbatical leave to study in Europe. The academic powers-that-be thought this to be okay, and a sabbatical was approved. Using this approval as an opening, Chamberlain was able to convince Bowdoin's president to let him serve the Union cause. Chamberlain enlisted as a private in the Union Army. Soon afterward, he obtained a commission from the governor of Maine. Two years later, he was a colonel commanding the Twentieth Maine Regiment in the Army of the Potomac.

On July 2, 1863, the Twentieth Maine was encamped near the little town of Gettysburg, Pennsylvania. The famous battle fought there was to become known as "the high point of the Confederacy." It is one of the bloodiest battles in American history. On the second day of fighting, the Twentieth Maine was assigned the mission of defending a wooded knoll known as Little Round Top. It was located on the extreme left end of the Union line. What the Federals didn't know was that Robert E. Lee had concentrated some fifteen thousand battle-hardened Confederates under Lieutenant General James "Old Pete" Longstreet to attack precisely on the left end of the Union line. If they could take Little Round Top, they could move their artillery to the knoll and fire along the unprotected Union line. This is called "enfiladed fire," and it is deadly. The Confederates could then have outflanked the entire Union line and cut off the Union troops in the center and on the right from their line of supplies.

Some military experts feel this action would have been decisive and that the Federals would have lost the battle. Because of previous Union defeats and other problems, the war had become extremely controversial and divisive in the North. England awaited a single decisive Confederate victory to recognize the Confederate States of America as an independent country. Had Longstreet been successful on that hot July afternoon, he might have ended not only the battle but the war. The United States of America might have been permanently divided into two countries.

Longstreet's Corps attacked with great determination and ferocity. The Twentieth Maine held. The Corps charged Little Round Top again. Once more, the Twentieth Maine beat them back. However, ammunition was running low; Chamberlain hoped that the Southerners would not attack again. Both sides had suffered greatly. Many Confederate dead and wounded marked the route of their previous assaults. But once again, the Confederates attacked. After a gallant effort, they were again forced to retreat. Chamberlain found that few of his troops had bullets left to shoot; they had no hope of resupply. There was nothing with which to defend the position against another Confederate onslaught.

Chamberlain's officers advised him to withdraw at once to prevent capture. He looked around at his battle-weary troops: the Twentieth Maine had suffered many casualties. Many of the survivors were wounded. The situation was critical; indeed, it seemed hopeless. "Tell the men to fix bayonets," Chamberlain ordered. His officers looked at him incredulously, but they carried out his orders. "Does the Colonel think he can scare off the attackers with a mere show of cold steel?" they thought. "What does he have in mind?" Yet his officers and soldiers knew that whatever he had in mind, he was totally committed. He had ordered fixed bayonets, and fix bayonets they did. Chamberlain looked down the hill toward the Confederate lines. He could see that Longstreet's men were forming their ranks for yet another attack. Chamberlain looked at his men. Pointing his saber at the grouping Confederates, he commanded, "Twentieth Maine . . . Charge!"

No tactics manuals advise an action like this. Still, the Twentieth Maine charged down from Little Round Top that day with bayonets fixed on their empty rifles. They yelled and screamed like madmen. The Confederates, brave as they were, fell back. Joshua Chamberlain's show of uncommon commitment and his use of redirection gave the Twentieth Maine the impetus to do the impossible. This act of redirection saved the entire battle of Gettysburg at a critical juncture.

Chamberlain was wounded several times during the Civil War. General Grant promoted him to brigadier general on what was thought to be Chamberlain's deathbed as he lay severely wounded. But he recovered to finish the war as a major general and help lead the victory parade of the Army of the Potomac, the largest of the Union armies, up Connecticut Avenue in Washington.

After the war, Chamberlain returned to Bowdoin College from his "sabbatical" and eventually became the college's president. He died from one of his old wounds, but not until he had reached the age of ninety-two. Joshua Chamberlain was a remarkable and Heroic Leader. In very real terms, his brilliant and courageous use of redirection—charging the enemy rather than surrendering—probably changed the course of history.[3]

Summary

Redirection should be considered when other influence tools don't work but when presenting the situation in a different way may well lead to success. There are three main points to remember when using redirection:

- Reframe perceptions of the situation in different terms.
- Focus on aspects that are more acceptable to those being led.
- Use imagination in developing this new presentation.

CHAPTER 12

. . . .

Deflection

. . . .

In using the deflection tool, the leader gets someone to do something by disclaiming the ability or power to do it. For example, an analyst goes to his supervisor and asks for help in doing some problems. "Gee, I'd like to help," the supervisor says, "but I haven't worked this type of analysis in quite a long time. How would you approach it? Why don't you begin. Maybe I'll remember a little." So the analyst begins to work on the problems. Whenever he gets stuck, his boss gets him going again. The supervisor is using the influence tool of deflection to get the analyst to learn to do the job.

Deflection can also be used by subordinates to lead their bosses, or by managers to lead other managers. "Boss, I have a problem, and I wonder how you would handle it." The boss is flattered to be asked. Many bosses are more than willing to help out. However, you must be careful to understand your boss when using this tool; some bosses prefer employees to work things out on their own (like the boss who used deflection himself in the first example). And you certainly don't want to overuse this tool.

Deflection can also be used as a tactic for not taking a certain action. During World War I General John J. Pershing commanded the American Expeditionary Force (AEF) in France. The United

States entered the war several years after their British and French allies, who of course had been in the war since the beginning, in 1914. The British and French had been fighting for three years, and their casualties had been tremendous. They saw the Americans as replacements for their losses. They proposed that the Americans not fight as a separate national unit but be distributed as replacements among the allied units already on the line. There were strong arguments for this approach: the Americans were inexperienced and could not be expected to be up to the standards of the battle-hardened allied forces.

Pershing knew that the American people would never accept their soldiers being used this way, but he could not make that argument to his British and French allies. Instead, he told his allies that his soldiers were accustomed to fighting together as Americans and that while they might not be effective at first, they would soon become acclimated. Furthermore, and more importantly, as commander of the AEF he did not have the authority to make this decision. Employing deflection, he said it was a political question and referred the allied commanders through their political channels to make their request of U.S. Secretary of War Newton Baker and President Woodrow Wilson. Of course, this was a setup, for Pershing knew that neither man would allow U.S. forces to be split up. The action allowed Pershing to get his way with his allies and avoid starting their relationship with a major rift. And he was right: the Americans soon proved themselves in battle, and the AEF made major contributions to the allied victory.[1]

Deflection and Sponsorship

When used with your boss, the deflection tool can lead to your getting support if as a result your boss becomes your mentor. Research of top managers both in and out of the military has discovered that no leader reaches the executive suite without a mentor or sponsor. A mentor is someone who has found a subordinate with special, useful ability and who keeps his eye on his protégé to help that person's career along. In some organizations mentoring has become systematized and has official status. General George C. Marshall carried mentoring to an art form in the military. He kept his own list of up-and-coming young officers and their qualifications. When World War II came, General Marshall was chief of staff of the Army. His knowledge and sponsorship of the young officers he had noticed years earlier led to the rapid elevation and promotion of men like Eisenhower, Bradley, Patton, and Mark Clark, all of whom were four- or five-star generals by the end of the war. Prior to the war, most had been junior lieutenant colonels.[2]

If you are going to use the deflection tool with your boss, you must be careful. You can use deflection to lead your boss, but do not expect automatic sponsorship. There is also the question of timing and individual preference; as I mentioned above, your boss may prefer that you work your problems out on your own. Finally, if you try to force the relationship, you're going to get in trouble with your boss as well as other managers at your level. Nobody likes what has variously been called a "teacher's pet," a "brown nose," or more kindly, a "fair-haired boy."

Many managers use the deflection tool to lead other managers at their level. Instead of competing in an area that the other manager does better, the good leader disclaims his own ability; in doing so, he gets his colleague to do what he wants. "Joe, you're the best softball coach the company team ever had. I'm going to recommend that you be named coach again this year."

Deflection and Sales

A long time ago I realized that a strong element of leadership is inherent in selling and that salespeople frequently use what I had previously thought of solely as leadership techniques. Automobile sales provides an excellent example, particularly in the use of the deflection tactic. Have you ever negotiated for a new automobile? You negotiate and negotiate. Finally, you come to a meeting of the minds and you think you have agreed on a final price. At that point the salesperson announces that he must have the price authorized by the sales manager, who is the only one with the final authority to close the deal. Fifteen minutes later he returns and tells you, "Good news! My manager approved the deal at only a few hundred dollars more."

When a salesperson pulls this on me, I always respond, "Gee, I'm afraid not. While you were gone, I called my wife. I always like to get her approval, and the best I can do is [several hundred dollars less than I had originally stated]." After all, if the dealership can change their final price, so can I. (By the way, this is why the salesperson will frequently ask even before you look at any cars whether you are prepared to buy today and whether you need to ask anyone else.) We usually end up at the price we had initially agreed to. And the salesperson never finds it necessary to get this price approved by the sales manager again. Now if you employ the deflection tool, you should do so ethically, for the benefit of those you lead or your mission, not to take advantage of anyone.

Deflection and Silence

When Generals Fogleman and Shelton jumped out of the C-17 to prove it safe for paratroopers, as narrated in Chapter Eight, their action was also an example, at the tactical level, of the use of deflection. If the C-17 had truly been unsafe to parachute from, they could have had it grounded until modifications were made. However, both knew that the aircraft was safe, despite rumors to the contrary. In setting the example they were also intimating that while they didn't have the power to do more (though they actually did), the aircraft was perfectly safe to parachute from.

Another air commander, who used the tool of deflection by setting the example without saying a word, was Jimmy Doolittle. As a lieutenant colonel, Doolittle led the first bombing raid of Japan early in World War II. Then they promoted him to general and sent him to Europe.

One of the airplanes they gave his airmen to fly was the B-26 "Marauder." There had been problems with the B-26. It was a difficult aircraft to fly. The airplane was known as a killer—of its own aircrew. So many were lost while in training in Florida that the airmen had a saying, "One a day in Tampa Bay."

In combat, there had been a reluctance to use the aircraft to its full potential. General Doolittle was faced with a situation where merely verbally rejecting the aircraft's bad reputation would not have worked. Tacitly deflecting his own official authority, he instead visited one of his B-26 groups and listened sympathetically to his pilots' complaints about the airplane. He then asked if he could fly one.

One of the pilots' beliefs was that if you lost an engine on takeoff, it was a sure thing you were going to roll over and crash back into the runway. On takeoff, Doolittle cut one of his engines. He made it off the ground safely and put the B-26 through all of its normal maneuvers—with only one engine. Then he landed the airplane, on one engine. Starting up the engine he had shut down, he took off again. This time he chopped the other engine, repeating all the maneuvers he had done previously. Finally, he landed on the single engine.

"Well," he told his pilots, "it isn't the easiest airplane to fly, but I think it can do the job pretty well." The B-26 went on to rack up an excellent operational record in combat during World War II.[3] General Doolittle became the highest-ranking reserve officer during World War II. After retirement, he was promoted again. He became the only the reserve officer ever promoted to four-star general.

Summary

It may seem strange that denying your own power can lead to accomplishing tasks that must be done, since much of what we hear is that leaders should present themselves as all-powerful and better equipped than everyone else to lead. But the results can be very effective. Keep the following basic facts in mind:

- You *can* frequently influence others to do things by denying your own ability.
- This influence tool can be used to influence not only subordinates but those at your level or higher.
- Setting the example may not only be a strategic move; it can also be used tactically to dispel a negative attitude toward something without saying a word.

CHAPTER 13

• •

Enlistment

• •

All you need to do is ask for help. That's the basis of enlistment as an influence tool. This tool is especially effective in situations where you don't have the power—or have the power but don't want to use it. Surprisingly, just asking works very well in more situations than you might think.

Psychologist Robert Cialdini looked at the motivation people used in influencing others to do things. In studying the literature on persuading through request, he found frequently that the request need not be phrased logically to gain a person's cooperation. Success may depend primarily on how the request is made and on the words used, rather than on the logic of the request itself. In one study that Cialdini analyzed, Harvard social psychologist Ellen Langer discovered that the number of people who would allow someone to get ahead of them in a line to make copies on an office copier depended primarily on a single word, even if the reason given for the request made no sense at all. If the requestor said, "Excuse me, I have five pages. May I use the Xerox machine because I am in a rush?" the positive response was 94 percent. That's pretty good. However, if the request was, "Excuse me, I have five pages. May I use the Xerox machine?" with no reason given, the positive response rate dropped to 60 percent. That's a sizeable drop, and before we go any further, it's pretty good evidence that we should give a reason why we want something done, time and circumstances permitting.

What is more, if the requestor phrased the request as, "Excuse me, I have five pages. May I use the Xerox machine because I have to make some copies?" you might expect the acceptance rate to remain pretty low—if the respondent didn't burst out laughing. After all, why else would someone ask to use a copier if not to make copies! Yet, as crazy as it sounds, the positive response was 93 percent, almost as high as if a real reason were given.[1] One interpretation of these results points to the use of the single word "because." The word alerted the respondent to a forthcoming explanation, even if the explanation itself was nonsense.

The point is that asking may be more powerful than you thought, as long as you give a reason for what you want done. However, allowing someone to get ahead in line is not much of a sacrifice. What happens if the request is a little more challenging?

Enlistment for Life-and-Death Tasks

Do you remember the television series *Baa Baa Black Sheep*? It told the story of Colonel Gregory "Pappy" Boyington, a Marine Corps fighter squadron commander, and his squadron during World War II. They called him "Pappy" because at the age of thirty-something he was the oldest member in the squadron. Pappy was in fact a real person, and the story of his successful leadership of his squadron in combat was true. Although some instances in the television series were fictional, the account I'm going to relate was real and was described in Colonel Boyington's autobiography (also titled *Baa Baa Black Sheep*). When the incident occurred, he was still a major, not a full colonel.

Boyington's story began when he was a Marine Corps fighter pilot on a Pacific island during World War II. He didn't have a combat job. He met a number of other Marine pilots who for one reason or another were in the same situation and had not been assigned flying duties. Most simply hadn't been trained as fighters; others were awaiting assignment. And others, like Boyington himself, were just plain misassigned: Boyington had actually flown in combat in China as one of General Claire Chennault's "Flying Tigers" and had shot down enemy aircraft. Of course, the television series made the situation more colorful by having each pilot grounded because of serious discipline problems and court-martialed for one offense or another. This was not true, but since the real pilots were unassigned or misassigned, they did consider themselves "Black Sheep," so that was the name eventually given to the members of their squadron.

One day, before there was a Black Sheep squadron, Boyington noticed a number of brand-new F4U Corsair aircraft parked near the runway and not in use. They were awaiting assignment to another fighter squadron still in training in the States. Boyington convinced his superiors to let him form an ad hoc squadron of volunteers to fly these airplanes while the other squadron was still en route. In the interim, Boyington trained his fliers and led them to become one of the best fighter squadrons in the theater. Eventually a permanent squadron, they were awarded the Presidential Unit Citation for extraordinary heroism in combat.

At one point, when the Black Sheep had been in combat for a fairly long time, they received word that the following day they would withdraw to a relatively safe island for rest and relaxation. Another squadron would fly their airplanes during this period. When the members of a combat squadron know that their last combat mission is over for a while, what happens? Having been in such a squadron myself, I can tell you that if it can, the squadron makes one huge party. The booze consumption goes up significantly. This is exactly what happened to the Black Sheep. When the last aircraft landed that evening, they began to party.

After hours of partying, most pilots retired for the night and went to sleep soundly, awaiting their departure in the morning.

Boyington himself was about ready to turn in when he received a message from headquarters on the main island. It was critical that he fly a night strafing mission before his squadron was flown to a rear area in the morning. He had no time to prepare. Right away he had to get four aircraft in the air and on their way to the target if they were going to strike and return in time to depart the next morning. Pappy Boyington didn't know what to do. His entire squadron had just concluded a huge party and consumed large quantities of alcohol. None were prepared psychologically to risk their lives in yet another combat mission before their R & R. How could he get them to do exactly that? How could any leader get his subordinates to do anything like this under such circumstances?

Here's what Pappy Boyington did, in his own words: "I walked up and down between the cots for some time, trying to think this thing out, occasionally looking at some of the nude bodies that were completely crapped out beneath the mosquito netting. These perspiring and motionless forms were dreaming of anything but a night strafing mission, I was positive. I didn't have the heart to order a flight, or to even ask the members who were assigned to my own flight to go with me.

"As I was thinking, I heard my own voice, not too loudly, and it said: 'Are there any three clowns dumb enough to want to strafe Kahili and Kara with me tonight?' " [2]

One of the Black Sheep looked up, blinked his eyes, and said, "I'll go with you, Pappy." Two others mumbled something like, "That sounds like fun."

Before he knew it, Boyington had his flight of four Black Sheep to do the job. They went out together, and they strafed the two targets. They went out on a dangerous combat mission, even though a couple hours earlier they had thought their combat was over for two weeks.

Pappy Boyington didn't give any better reason for strafing Kahili and Kara than the researcher did in asking to make photocopies. And a night combat mission was certainly a lot more dangerous than making copies on a Xerox machine. Still, Boyington's Black Sheep followed. Will such enlistment always work? Of course not. But it *can* work, and just as a doctor must sometimes try different medicines before finding the right one, the leader must do the same.

Making the Enlistment Tool Work

Boyington's success in using the enlistment tool illustrates several elements that are important, even necessary for the tool to work. First, he didn't give any orders. Nobody *had* to do this. Those who came with him were volunteers. Next, Boyington didn't send them out on this hazardous mission. He led them himself. Finally, he made this difficult and challenging job fun. Look at how he worded his request: "Are there any three clowns dumb enough to want to strafe Kahili and Kara with me tonight?" He implied that the job was to be a "lark." He wanted three "clowns" who were as "dumb" as he was to pull a stunt like this. The impression was that he was going to go out and have some fun: Who wanted to join him? Yet this mission was deadly serious. It had been ordered by a higher headquarters which was well aware that the entire squadron had probably been partying. The mission was clearly important for the military effort. Yet Boyington mentioned none of these things. He didn't try to convince his men that the mission was needed or to persuade them in any way. Persuasion is another important influence tool and the topic of Chapter Fourteen. It probably wouldn't have been as effective in this case. A look at each of the elements in Boyington's handling of this situation shows why simply enlisting was the preferred influence tool in this instance.

Volunteers

When you enlist someone to do something, you are asking them to volunteer. Boyington did not want to order anyone on this mission, and not only because it was dangerous. He had ordered many dangerous missions previously. This mission was different: his pilots had already "done their duty" and flown combat during the day. Moreover, they'd been told that their dangerous work was over for two weeks and that nothing more was required of them until the end of that period. Finally, they were tired, and not at their best due to their earlier party. Boyington had no time to prepare. Had there been any other possibilities, he would have made them clear to those at headquarters. But he knew that the mission had to be flown and that no other unit was available to do it. He could have ordered the mission flown, and it would have been flown; yet he knew that the pilots' state of mind would then be negative and resentful. When embarking on a difficult task, you want those who follow you to be positive and confident, not negative and resentful.

During the Cuban Missile Crisis, I was assigned to a B-52 crew. For almost a month we were on airborne or ground alert, as all training missions were deferred for the duration. During the twenty-four- to twenty-seven-hour airborne alert flights, which were armed with nuclear weapons, we were able to have one pilot and one navigator on duty while another rested. Then we landed and were sent home for twenty-four hours, followed by ground alert for a couple of days to recover. That was the norm. However, after one airborne alert flight, as the crew bus took us to debriefing, our aircraft commander told us that because of various contingencies we would get only a couple of hours' rest and then would immediately launch on a second twenty-four- to twenty-seven-hour alert flight. We would not be permitted to return home.

I remember the feelings of resentment when we heard this order. Our aircraft commander had been given this information well before the time of our first flight. He could have told us then. He might have used the enlistment tool and asked us to volunteer for the second flight. All would have readily done so. We would have had the chance to inform our families that we would be gone for several days and to make other personal plans. We would have had time to prepare mentally and pace ourselves during our first flight. Instead, we had very little time. We were angry. Not all of us were able to reach our families, and this was before the day of answering machines. These individuals had to rely on others to inform the family that they wouldn't be coming home. We obeyed orders, but we didn't much like it. Though we followed through and performed our duty as ordered, we might have performed much more efficiently and effectively and with a much better attitude had a different influence tool been used.

Getting Out in Front

Chapter Eight discussed how effective leading by example and getting out in front can be. Getting out in front is especially important when you are leading by enlistment. There is an old saying that as a leader you must never ask someone to do something you are unwilling to do yourself. In an era of high technology this is not always possible. You may be willing to design a complicated computer program, but if you don't have the knowledge or training, you simply aren't able to do the job. Nevertheless, when you use the enlistment tool, you must be prepared to get out in front of the project in any way you can. Pappy Boyington was perfectly capable of flying the night combat mission, and it probably never entered his mind not to lead it. In fact, the basis of his appeal at enlistment was, "Are there any three clowns dumb enough to want to strafe Kahili and Kara *with me* tonight?" Had he not been capable of leading this mission, it would have been far more difficult to use the enlistment tool. He might have been forced to use some other influence tool or have approached the problem in another way. For example, he might have awakened his second in command, explained the situation to him, and then said something like, "I just bet Jim $400 that he is too soused to attack Kahili and Kara tonight. Are there any three clowns dumb enough to want to strafe Kahili and Kara with him?" The point is, when using enlistment, the leader is far more effective when actually leading, or at least when he has some personal stake in the matter.

Making Challenging Work Fun

Every day, people take up difficult and challenging work voluntarily, no matter how difficult or dangerous. Why? Because they have decided that what they are doing is not work; it's fun. Why else do hunters get up before dawn in the freezing cold, sit shivering uncomfortably for hours hidden behind a camouflaged blind awaiting game, and sometimes return hours later with nothing to show for their efforts? Certainly not for the food, money, or any other gain. Why do some people jump off of bridges attached to a bungee line? Or parachute out of an airplane, or play a sport in which injuries are frequent, or climb mountains? Are people crazy? Not at all. Even the most challenging, difficult, and dirtiest work will not only be gladly taken up, it will be sought after—if that work is considered fun by those who engage in it. That's why kids will sometimes do something we adults consider just plain stupid and dangerous. And well it may be, but the kids consider it fun. Boyington appealed to these emotions. He's didn't say that the mission was critical or that it had been ordered by higher headquarters. He implied that it was contrary to what headquarters would have approved, and that it would be a lark. It would be fun.

Summary

Enlistment is another valuable influence tool in leadership. It works best for the Heroic Leader when

- It is voluntary.
- The leader leads.
- It is fun.

CHAPTER 14

• •

Persuasion

• •

Persuasion differs from enlistment in one important way. With enlistment, all you need do is ask. Of course, asking in a dramatic or creative way helps. With persuasion, however, the emphasis isn't on asking. You must actually convince someone to do something, and that requires providing reasons and rationale.

Using Persuasion

We might think that a leader always has a great deal of authority with which to lead. This frequently isn't true. My friend and fellow West Point graduate Colonel Jack Gillette commanded fighter squadrons for years. As a squadron commander, Jack had a lot of authority. He commanded his fighter pilots, and they did what he told them to do. Of course, he didn't always use direction in his leadership, but he had the authority to give his men orders and to have them obeyed.

Then, in 1969, Jack was assigned as program manager for the development and testing of the F/FB-111, a new airplane that came in two versions. One was the straight fighter version, the F-111. The other, designated the FB-111, was a bomber used by Strategic Air Command.

Along with the two versions Jack had two groups of pilots flying airplanes for his program. Each group reported to a different Air Force colonel. Neither of these colonels reported to Jack! The fighter colonel reported to a general in Tactical Air Command; the bomber colonel reported to a general in Strategic Air Command. Jack, in Air Force Systems Command, was in charge of the F/FB-111 test program. He told me that the only group he actually commanded consisted of a secretary and one administrative sergeant.

As Jack told me, "It's a real test of my leadership. When I want a test flight made, I can't order a single pilot into the air. I have to persuade either the fighter or bomber commander who has authority over these pilots to do it."

Jack was successful because he is a superb leader. His dilemma, however, was not unique. It is familiar to tens of thousands of program managers in government and industry across the country. These leaders have authority over their programs, but no authority or limited authority over many of the people who work on those programs.

Besides being your main option when you have no power, persuasion can also work well when leading others who have comparable power or more power in the situation than you have. This is especially true when you have no way of rewarding or punishing someone. Let's say you are the leader of a group of volunteers, or must get other leaders at your level to follow you. Maybe you must induce a group of your superiors to follow your lead. In all of these situations, consider persuasion as an influence tactic for getting others to follow your lead.

Logic

What means can you use to implement the persuasion tactic? One way is to convince through logic. Simply give the person you want to persuade good reasons for doing what you want.

Everyone wants to know why they are being asked to do a certain thing. This is true whether you have authority over them or not. My feeling is that you owe this to those you would have follow you. And giving your reasons has an important fringe benefit. When the situation changes and you aren't available to give new instructions, people will know what you were trying to accomplish; they can alter their actions according to your reasons for taking the actions in the first place. You will find that you and your organization will be more successful at reaching goals than would otherwise be the case.

Personal Need

Another way of using the persuasion tactic is to emphasize your personal need or the worthiness of your cause. A young engineer once wound up leading his unit's savings-bond drive. It was the sort of unfamiliar assignment that could have turned into a disaster, but he succeeded brilliantly and proved himself as a leader. Of course, he talked to his unit about competing with other company units, and he also spoke about the advantages of savings bonds. But in addition he spoke of his personal need to do well as a new employee with the responsibility for heading up the bond campaign.

People selling door-to-door often emphasize their personal need for the sale: they're working their way through college or competing for a scouting award or the like. These examples of persuasion emphasize personal need. They are used because they work.

Persuasion and Time Pressure

Usually, persuasion is reserved for situations where the would-be leader has the time to explain the case and the argument for doing what needs to be done. However, this isn't always possible, especially in situations that call for Heroic Leadership.

Harry DeWolf was a Canadian naval officer in command of the destroyer HMCS *St. Laurent* when he observed a sailor painting an armed torpedo. Much to his horror and before he could stop him, the sailor first lifted the safety catch to paint underneath it, and then lifted the firing handle to paint under that. The torpedo fired and ran wild on deck. According to DeWolf, "It slammed into the deck house, bounced off and kept charging around. Everybody, including me, was scared." In seconds, the decks cleared. As soon as the torpedo had gone a sufficient distance and was fully armed, it would strike something and blow up, killing everyone within range. It was obvious to DeWolf that the only way to stop it was to grab it and hold on. But it was too much for one man. DeWolf turned to the nearest seaman, a petty officer by the name of Ridge, and persuaded him to help grab it. He used the persuasion tool, but his persuasive argument was pretty short: "This is our only chance."

DeWolf continues: "It was as slippery as a greased pig and we thought its propeller might cut our feet off. We rode and guided it over the rail and stuck one leg over the rail to hold it steady. The propeller was making a tremendous racket on the iron deck. We finally managed to release the air cock (the torpedo was driven by compressed air). We still had a live torpedo. When we got to port (in the United Kingdom) we hoisted it on the wall and left it there. I reported to headquarters, but I don't know what became of the torpedo."[1] Admiral DeWolf was acknowledged as the most decorated British Commonwealth naval officer of World War II. Eventually he became a vice admiral and chief of the Canadian Naval Staff. Few knew that despite numerous naval engagements during which he displayed great heroism, Admiral DeWolf suffered from seasickness throughout his career.

Persuasion in Business

Joe Karbo had only two years of college, but he was a successful entrepreneur. His college education had been interrupted by World War II, and he quit the University of Southern California in Los Angeles to take up arms for Uncle Sam. After the war, Joe went into advertising. Then television caught on; by the late 1950s there was one in almost every American home. Joe noticed that on at least one channel in Los Angeles a lot of advertising opportunity was going to waste. Every night at 12:30 the "Star-Spangled Banner" would play, and the screen would go to static, ending the broadcast for the day. Joe approached the owners and negotiated for that time block—all night, from 12:30 until 7:00, when broadcasting resumed.

Joe didn't have the money to run a full night of broadcasting, so he approached five investors to put up the money that would allow him to invest in his project. He then started a talk show, ran movies, and arranged for different entertainers to come to the studio and perform live before the television cameras. He sold the advertising time. Before he knew it, he was taking in money hand over fist, as much as $50,000 a week—quite a lot of money for those days. For many months his cash flow allowed him to meet his bills and pay back the money he had borrowed.

One evening, when he walked in to begin his nightly programming, he was greeted by a stranger. Unknown to him, the station had been sold, and the new owners were taking over the operation to do their own broadcasting and sell the time themselves from the first night. Joe was desperate. He owed his creditors $25,000. He didn't have any other source of income, and he couldn't pay back the money he owed. His creditors threatened to sue him. He contacted a lawyer who examined all the facts and told him that he had no option. If he wanted to avoid a costly lawsuit that he was bound to lose, he had no choice but to declare bankruptcy.

Joe thought it over. He didn't want to declare bankruptcy. He knew that he owed individuals money and that they should be paid. Moreover, he realized that if he ever wanted to start another business and needed to raise money, having a bankruptcy on his record would make things very difficult. Finally, he realized that as far as the investment group was concerned, he was its leader, even if the group was dissatisfied with his present leadership. Instead of declaring bankruptcy, Joe decided to use persuasion.

Calling the group together, he told them essentially this: He did not have the money to pay them back. It was true that it was his responsibility, as he had failed to anticipate that the station might be sold and that he had no contract protecting him from being replaced by new owners who wished to do their own broadcasting. If the investors forced him to declare bankruptcy, they would get perhaps 10 percent of their money back at best. Joe had no intention of running out on them and paying them anything less than the full amount that he owed them. Although he didn't have a job or other source of income, he did have a skill: he had learned how to sell useful products directly to prospective customers. If they would allow him to invest the remaining money, he proposed a reduced payment schedule that would extend the time before they would receive the full amount they were owed, but they would receive every penny. In the end, this leader persuaded his followers, a group of investors, to agree to his proposal.

Through the use of persuasion as an influence tool, Karbo was able to sell various products to customers. He paid off the money he owed his investors within two years through sales of a single product, which he sold directly to businessmen through the mail. The successful product that allowed him to pay off his debts in such a short period was a little booklet—of which he sold 250,000 copies—titled "How to Avoid Bankruptcy." A few years later, Karbo became internationally famous when he sold thirteen million copies of another booklet in eleven languages through a newspaper advertisement. It was called "The Lazy Man's Way to Wealth."

Summary

- Like enlistment, persuasion requires the leader to ask for something. The major difference is that the leader must actually justify his reasons and convince his followers.

- Persuasion is useful in situations where you have limited authority, especially when those you lead have comparable or even greater power than you.

- Although more difficult to employ when time is short, if your reasons are clear and concise, persuasion can still be used.

- Recognize that in many situations you are the leader, even if you don't have *leader* in your title; in such situations, persuasion is a key tool.

CHAPTER 15

● ●

Negotiation

● ●

With negotiation you influence by conferring with others to arrive at a settlement that you (and the others) find acceptable. It may involve compromise and usually entails trading something that the other side wants or wants done for what you want done. You may never have imagined negotiation as an influence element of leadership, but it is. Negotiation may be required under certain circumstances. Does what you want offer little or no perceived benefit to the person you want to influence? Do you and those you want to lead have about equal power? Can both sides help or hurt each other almost equally? If any of these conditions exist, you may find the negotiation tool extremely useful.

For example, in a university the addition of new courses must be voted on by all departments. New course offerings may be perceived as attracting students from one department to another; thus there may be no reason for one department to vote for another department's proposal for a new course. If you want to get the university to offer a new course, part of your leadership may require using a negotiation tactic. How can you do this? You could offer to support another department's proposal for a new course. Or you could offer something else the other department wants in exchange for its support for your proposal.

Negotiation in War

Is negotiation ever a part of Heroic Leadership? Most certainly. It is necessary and used frequently when different types of forces such as soldiers, sailors, airmen, and Marines are employed together. It is also used when forces of more than one nation are employed in combined operations. For example, George Washington used negotiation successfully in a key battle for winning America's independence.

By the summer of 1781 the British strength was divided into two strongholds: New York and Chesapeake Bay. The Americans' French allies had a contingent of the French Army with General Washington under General Jean Rochambeau. British forces were stronger than the combined American-French force. But the combined allied force was stronger than either British force if faced separately. If the two British forces could be cut off from each other, they could be defeated individually.

The French had a strong fleet under the command of Admiral Francois de Grasse. Now the hurricane season started in late summer and grew progressively worse into the fall. De Grasse did not want to get involved in a campaign in the north for fear of having his fleet destroyed at sea by these storms.

Washington's original plans called for defeating the British in the Chesapeake Bay area and then moving south for an attack on Charleston or the British base at Wilmington. He got de Grasse to support him by using a negotiating strategy. Washington told the admiral, "If you sail north and can keep command of the sea during my operations against the Chesapeake Bay force, you can return to the West Indies immediately thereafter." In another words, Washington let de Grasse off the hook for supporting other allied operations that year in return for his immediate services against the British Chesapeake Bay forces. De Grasse answered that his fleet would be available until mid-October.

On August 30, de Grasse's fleet arrived off Yorktown, Virginia. He also brought reinforcements and siege artillery. More important, he took command of the sea and isolated the British land forces under Lord Cornwallis. Six weeks later Cornwallis surrendered. The Battle of Yorktown is known as the decisive battle of the War of Independence. The British opened peace negotiations the following spring.[1]

Knowledge—of Desire—Is Power

The essence of negotiation is, "If you do this, I'll do something else in return." Of course, you well know what you want done. It is critical that you understand what the individual or group you are trying to lead wants. You must offer something of value to them. George Washington understood that what mattered most to Admiral de Grasse was avoiding the loss of his ships to known weather conditions, so he based the "reward" on eliminating this risk and was successful in getting de Grasse to employ his ships in support of Washington's plan.

Sometimes what others want is well known and obvious. At other times this is not the case. For example, I once did a study for a major aerospace company on its performance in winning or losing relatively small—that is, under $2 million—research and development contracts with the U.S. government. The corporate engineers who bid these contracts were convinced that low price was the key, and their prices were almost always lower than their competitors'. They even pointed out that published U.S. government policy was to go with low-price bids unless a higher price was beneficial to the government, and higher prices had to be justified. The problem was, the company lost as many contracts as they won.

In investigating this issue, I found that while it was true that the government was normally required to contract with the lowest bidder, the primary thing the government was interested in was a successful outcome to their investment in these small research and development efforts. While the government's perception of these outcomes was based on a number of factors, a major one was the quantity and quality of contacts made by the contractor with government representatives before the contract was ever bid. Through these contacts the government gained confidence in the contractor's proposed approach to the effort and that its people fully understood the problem. By the time the contract was actually bid, the government was far more confident of a successful outcome. This company's offer had been "You give us the contract; in return we'll give you the lowest price" when it should have been "You give us the contract; in return you will have high confidence in a successful outcome." The company significantly increased its win-loss ratio by adjusting its preproposal marketing efforts to increase the quantity and quality of contacts made with the government.

Using Reward as an Incentive

Rewards of all types can be an incentive used in negotiation, even though you may never call your dialogue with those you lead a negotiation.

During World War I, General Douglas MacArthur was a thirty-eight-year-old brigadier general. He had been in combat for some time and had just assumed command of a new brigade in France. In those days soldiers wore their medals, even on their combat uniforms, and one that General MacArthur wore was the Distinguished Service Cross (a high award for valor, second only to the Congressional Medal of Honor). After planning an important attack, he went forward and waited in the trenches with the battalion (about a thousand soldiers) that was going to lead the way. This battalion had never been in combat, much less made an attack of this type. He could see that the young battalion commander was nervous. Yet in a very few minutes they were going to go "over the top," that is, climb out of the trench that protected them and go forward under fire toward the enemy lines.

MacArthur called the battalion commander to him. "Major," he said, "when the signal comes to go over the top, if you go first, before your men, your battalion will follow you. Moreover, they will never doubt your leadership or courage in the future."

Now normally, a battalion commander was not supposed to lead an attack from the front. The military tactics manuals said that a battalion commander should be with the company following the company in the lead. That way he was not as vulnerable and could better control the attack as it unfolded. But MacArthur knew that there are times when the rules must be violated, and this was one.

"I will not order you to do this," continued MacArthur. "In the front of the battalion, every German gun will be trained on you. It will be very dangerous and require a great deal of courage. However, if you do it, you will earn the Distinguished Service Cross—and I will see that you get it."

Very few were awarded the Distinguished Service Cross, and it is held in very high esteem by all soldiers. Looking at MacArthur's comments, it is clear that this moment was actually a negotiation: if you lead the attack from the front (which I want), I will see that you receive a Distinguished Service Cross (which you want).

MacArthur then stepped back and looked the major over for several long moments. He stepped forward again. "I see you are going to do it. So you will have the Distinguished Service Cross right now." So saying, MacArthur unpinned his own Distinguished Service Cross from his uniform and pinned it on the uniform of the major.

What happened when the signal came to go over the top? It is of course no surprise that the major, proudly wearing a Distinguished Service Cross (which he had not yet actually earned), charged out in front of his troops. And as MacArthur had forecast, his troops followed behind him. They were successful in securing their objective.[2]

Note that although MacArthur clearly declared his objectives and what he expected, he gave no direct orders. Instead, he employed the negotiation tool to get the major to do what was needed to ensure a successful attack.

Summary

You can apply negotiation in many ways to lead all types of organizations. To make negotiation successful,

- Know clearly what you want.
- Make sure that what you offer in return is valued by those you want to lead.
- Never, never renege on your agreement; if you do, you will lose all respect and trust of those you lead.

CHAPTER 16

● ●

Involvement

● ●

If you can get others involved in what you want done, they will adopt your goal as their own and become committed to its attainment. Because of this, involvement is a powerful influence tactic. It can usually be combined fairly easily with one or more of the tools discussed in previous chapters. Involvement is part of a major element in how the Japanese manage. The Japanese call the technique *ringi*. Under *ringi* Japanese leaders take extraordinary pains to ensure that leaders and workers at all levels have an input into a proposed action. Until everyone has had an opportunity to study and comment on the proposal, no action is taken. Executives from other countries who do business with the Japanese sometimes get extremely frustrated with *ringi*. Decisions that would take days in the United States may take months in Japan. But once the decision is made, the entire Japanese organization is involved and is committed to a successful outcome. The organization then implements the decision amazingly quickly and effectively. In comparison, decisions made in American organizations are sometimes taken quickly but then turn out to be difficult to implement. The reason is that many members of the American organization are neither involved in the action nor committed to the goal.

Ownership of Ideas

Why is involvement so important? One dimension is ownership. We work and fight much harder for things that are our own. As a corollary to this, ideas from someone else do not become our own instantaneously. Dr. Chester Karrass has devoted much of his life to the science of negotiation and has written several important books on the subject. If you've flown the airlines, it would be hard to miss his advertisements or his slogan: "In business, you don't get what you deserve, you get what you negotiate."

In his seminars and tapes Karrass cautions us to allow enough time when introducing new ideas. "Introducing ideas," he says, "is like introducing new friends. It takes time to know and understand people before someone else's friends become our friends as well. Therefore, when you introduce new ideas to someone else, you must give them sufficient time to get to know them before you can expect agreement." Involving people succeeds as an influence tactic because it gives them ownership. But you need to allow sufficient time for ownership to develop.

Three Subsets of Involvement

One researcher found three important subsets of using involvement to influence others:[1]

- Sharing
- Enabling
- Cooperating

All three have to do with building on the ideas of others. You do this in such a way that your ideas, contacts, or other resources and those of the people you lead are pooled and exchanged. You share your thoughts and enable them to come up with ideas of their own. Through cooperation, something greater results that neither you nor those you lead could come up with alone.

Please note that sharing information with others is exactly opposite to the way many people mistakenly try to lead. Such leaders hoard information and refuse to share it with anyone. They seem to think that if they keep information to themselves, they will look smarter than those they would have follow them. How wrong they are! When you are the leader, it is those who follow you that make you look smart—or not.

If people make errors and look bad because they are missing information you could have given them, you will ultimately suffer far more than they. It is you, and no one else, who are responsible for everything your organization does or fails to do.

Involving Others When You Have No Authority

You may think that military leaders have the authority of military law to enforce their orders. "Leading in civilian life is a lot different," you may think. An executive in a company doesn't have that kind of authority. In the rest of the chapter, we'll look at a situation where a leader had no authority.

Leading informal teams is sometimes really difficult. The leader has limited authority; many decisions can only be taken with the consent of others. Similarly, others lead teams in "matrix organizations"; they control the budget for the program but pay for staff who report not to them but to a functional manager. In both situations, leading is harder because the leader has limited authority. Some leadership situations are even more challenging: the leader may have no authority at all. Fortunately, the involvement tool works in many different situations, especially when the leader has limited authority or lacks even a formal organization.

Let me tell you about my friend Joe Cossman. He passed away several years ago, but he made millions of dollars without a college education thanks to his outstanding leadership—and his frequent use of involvement.

During World War II, Cossman served in the Combat Engineers in Europe. After the war, with no formal education, he got a job working for an import company in Pittsburgh, Pennsylvania. His pay (converted to today's dollars) was $350 a week. On this small paycheck Joe supported his wife, a baby daughter, and himself.

After hours, Joe worked part time from his kitchen table trying to find products made in the United States for export to Europe. He had little success for a year. Then one day he saw a small classified ad in the *New York Times*. It was for laundry soap, which at the time was in short supply overseas. Joe answered the ad, got samples, and sent them to several overseas contacts. Almost by return mail he received an order with a letter of credit for $1,800,000 (also converted to today's dollars).

The letter of credit said that a New York bank would pay him this fabulous sum as soon as he turned over bills of lading—documents showing the product on a ship bound for the buyer. There was also a deadline. The bills of lading had to be presented to the bank within thirty days or the letter of credit would be worthless. This protected the buyers from having their money tied up indefinitely.

An "Impossible" Leave of Absence

Cossman went to see his boss and asked for a leave of absence. The boss told Joe it was impossible—this was their busiest season. Joe couldn't afford to quit his $350-a-week job. Somebody had to make a trip to New York to close the deal. He asked almost everyone he knew in Pittsburgh to go for him. He offered them half of the profits. All declined.

Finally, Joe went to his boss again. He showed uncommon commitment in doing this, but what was more important, he got his boss emotionally involved in the project. This time his boss said yes. Joe withdrew his life savings from the bank. It was a few hundred dollars. Then he left for New York.

Joe picks up the story: "When I got to New York, I telephoned the man who ran the ad. The man didn't own a single bar of soap! He had put the ad in the paper on speculation and sent samples he had bought in a store." Despite this setback, Joe didn't give up. He went to the New York Public Library and got the names and addresses of every soap manufacturer in the United States. The next day he locked himself in his hotel room and started to make a call. Now another big problem reared up: it seems there was a telephone strike. It took fifteen minutes before he finally got a manager who was acting as an operator. Joe immediately told the manager his story and got him involved. Cossman had page after page of telephone numbers to call. Influenced by Joe's commitment and his own involvement in the project, the operator agreed to help him. He promised to keep Joe on the line until he had made all of his calls.

After fifty calls with no positive results, Joe fell into bed exhausted. "When the sun came up, I began again. I had to tell my story all over again to the new operator-manager. She also stayed with me to help me make my calls." When a leader is really committed and gets followers involved, they rarely quit. At noon, he finally hit pay dirt. He found a company in Alabama that had laundry soap. Joe had racked up a telephone bill approaching a thousand dollars, but he had located the product.

Joe continues, "I was so excited, I told them I would fly to Alabama that afternoon. They told me to save my money. Their corporate offices were only a few blocks away in Rockefeller Center."

Involving the Company President

Joe ran all the way. Before long he was telling his story to the president of the soap company. He completed the deal with no cash, but with his inexperience, he made a mistake: Joe took delivery of the soap in Alabama, not New York City. It was his responsibility to get the soap to New York.

"I began pounding the pavements of New York. I looked for a company president that would loan me thirty trucks and drivers on credit. It took two days. I finally found a president of a trucking company willing to take his trucks to Alabama even though I had no money to pay in advance." How did Joe pull this off? You guessed it, the involvement tool again.

Joe no longer had a cent to his name. During the trip he borrowed money for meals from the truck drivers. They finally arrived in Alabama and loaded a thousand cases of soap on the trucks. They immediately turned around and headed back to New York. But time was running out.

"We arrived in New York twenty-four hours before the letter of credit was due to expire. They started loading the soap on the 'lighters' which took the cargo to the freighters in the harbor. The unions weren't as strong in those days, and I persuaded the longshoreman to let me help." Joe worked all night helping to load the soap and through the next day until noon.

At noon, he looked at the boxes yet to be loaded and realized he wasn't going to make it. He wouldn't get his "on board" bills of lading to give to the bank until it was too late. The banks closed at two o'clock, only two hours away. His letter of credit would then be worthless.

The offices of the steamship line were near the docks. Cossman found the president's office and barged his way into the president's suite. He hadn't washed or changed clothes in a week. "I thought I might have made good use of a case of my own soap," he told me. First he got the president's secretary involved. She told the president there was a man that wanted to see him; he was pretty strange looking, but she thought he should hear his story. Involvement again. Then he saw the president, and once more he used the involvement tool. "If you've gone this far, you're not going to lose the deal now," the president said.

The steamship line president pushed a few buttons on his desk, and people appeared from nowhere. Within minutes Joe had his bills of lading. This was a risk to the steamship line, because their insurance didn't begin until the soap was on the ship. The president even sent his limousine to take Joe to the bank.

Joe got to the bank just fifteen minutes before closing time. He rushed in and presented his bills of lading. "The teller gave me a check for $1,800,000, and I went outside to get a taxi. Only then did I remember that though I had a check for $1,800,000, I didn't have taxi fare to get back to my hotel." He went back into the bank, which fortunately hadn't closed, and got checks for all his creditors—and some cash.

Cossman went on to build a multimillion-dollar corporation. His company sold dozens of unusual products, from "Fisherman Joe's" fishing lures (250,000 sold) to ant farms for children (1.8 million sold). His employees, and others outside his company, never failed to follow Joe's lead. He always got them involved in some way with his projects. Moreover, as Joe simply would not quit, neither would anyone else he became involved with, though he frequently had no authority over them whatsoever.

Summary

Involvement is one of the most powerful influence tools because it helps those that follow adopt the leader's goals as their own. Using a popular term, followers become "engaged." To use this tool effectively, here's what you should remember:

- Involvement is useful in many types of situations.
- Get the individuals you want to influence interested and invested in your project. Once they "own" your goals, their commitment will follow naturally.
- Sharing information and resources, enabling others to contribute ideas, and cooperating together are key elements of creating involvement.
- Involvement will help you to lead when you have no authority over others.

PART THREE

The Eight Competencies of Heroic Leadership

You don't need to master special competencies to simply lead, but you do if you aspire to be a Heroic Leader. Heroic Leaders do things that ordinary leaders won't or can't do. Here are the eight competencies that make the difference:

- Attracting followership
- Developing self-confidence
- Building a heroic team
- Developing high morale and esprit de corps
- Motivating people when times get tough
- Taking charge in crisis situations
- Developing charisma
- Solving problems and making decisions

Fasten your seat belt—in the following chapters you will begin building the competencies you will need to be a Heroic Leader of any team.

CHAPTER 17

• •

How to Attract Followership

• •

No one follows anyone else without being motivated to do so. Look at any situation where men and women follow a leader and you will discover reasons for their doing so. Luck or unusual circumstances may play a part. But mostly followers respond to definite actions the leader takes. In this chapter you will learn actions you must take to motivate others to follow you.

Make Others Feel Important

Everyone wants to feel important, from the youngest child to the oldest grandparent. After basic survival it is one of the most important of human needs. It is frequently the real reason behind a child's tantrum or an adult's rudeness. A recent television special sought the reason that some children become school-ground bullies. Why do some children insist on dominating and threatening their playmates? Why do some children torment and persecute other children? Sociologists figured that bullies would be less intelligent; they thought these would be the kids who couldn't do well in class. In most cases this just wasn't true.

What they did discover was that bullies got a sense of importance by lording it over others. As one former bully, now grown up, told television viewers, "The more I was able to make weaker kids do what I wanted, the more important I felt." But this same motivator, feeling important, can have a tremendously powerful and positive effect when applied properly by Heroic Leaders.

Toward the end of the Civil War, General Robert E. Lee faced a force of one hundred thousand Union troops with only thirty thousand of his own. Just as he was about to be overrun, the Texas Brigade, commanded by General John Gregg, showed up. As related by Alf J. Mapp Jr., "Lee rode up to the front of the brigade, stood in his stirrups, raised his hat from his head and boomed above the martial din, 'Texans always move them.' An ear-splitting yell rose from the brigade. One of Gregg's couriers, with tears running down his cheeks, shouted, 'I would charge hell itself for that old man!'"[1]

General Courtney Whitney was with General MacArthur for more than twenty years. When asked what made MacArthur great, he replied, "He made his men feel that their contribution was an important one—that they were somebody."[2]

That sense of importance is frequently more powerful as a motivator than money, promotion, working conditions, or almost anything else. So we do everything possible to make others feel important. Right? Wrong. We do the exact opposite. When we meet a surly clerk, we don't think, "This person needs to feel important, and I'm going to help build that feeling." Oh no, not us! We think, "How dare this person talk that way to me. I'll make it clear who's really important around here."

We find ourselves playing a game of one-upmanship in rudeness. And the results are perfectly predictable. We have what is sometimes referred to in the military as a "pissing contest." If we have more power than the other person, we will probably get our way. The subordinate will put up with our tirade and probably won't argue with us. But at what cost? Analysts term this style of mis-leadership "manager disrespect." Professor Jack Mendleson at Bethel College in Mishawaka, Indiana, writes, "Preliminary research findings show that manager disrespect has reached an epidemic level in the U.S."[3] Many so-called leaders don't lead. They confront and dominate with manager disrespect.

When you lapse into manager disrespect, you may or may not succeed. One thing, however, is certain: the person you are doing this to will not appreciate it. You may not be able to trust that person to follow your lead or your intentions if you aren't around in the future. In fact, if I had to bet money, I would wager on the exact opposite. I'm not saying there aren't times when you must let someone know you are dissatisfied about something done or left undone. But don't belittle someone's importance so that they lose their self-respect—not if you want to lead and influence them.

Treat Others as You Would Be Treated Yourself

Both the Old and New Testaments tell us to treat others as we want to be treated ourselves. You may have thought this concept has application only in religious or ethical conduct. The truth is that it also has a great deal to do with good leadership. Why? Because people do not willingly follow someone who is unconcerned with how they are treated. Mary Kay Ash, the woman who built a billion-dollar corporation while giving away pink Cadillacs to her most successful saleswomen, called this her "Golden Rule System of Management." She not only practiced it herself; she recommended it to everyone in her organization.

After all, what makes you so special? Do you think you are so much better than others that you ought to be treated differently? If so, you'd better change your way of thinking, or you may never get people to follow you.

The best of today's corporate leaders have discovered that it is simply good leadership to treat family issues as strategic business issues, and to make the welfare of their employees' families a major priority. At First Tennessee National Corporation, this started with CEO Ralph Horn in the 1990s. Horn dumped the old work rules and let employees figure out which schedules worked best from their families' viewpoint. Then he added a host of new programs to help the families of his employees. He sent his one thousand managers to three and a half days of training to educate them and get them on board. That certainly made them feel important. Results? Productivity and customer service soared, and high retention rates contributed to a 55 percent profit gain in two years.[4] And these policies continue to affect Tennessee National Corporation years later. This company is part of a currently most unpopular industry: banking. Nevertheless, here are awards it has received as I write in 2009: Best Employers in Tennessee, *Business Tennessee Magazine*, 2009; Top 50 Companies for Executive Women, National Association of Female Executives, 2009; Grand Prix Award, Best Overall Investor Relations and Best Investor Relations Officer, *IR Magazine*, small cap category, 2009.[5]

If you really want to be a Heroic Leader, put the interest of those you are privileged to lead even above your own. Followers want leaders who protect their interests, not the leaders'. Few situations require you to sacrifice your own life for those you lead, but that is exactly what Sergeant First Class Paul Smith did in Iraq when his men came under attack by a superior enemy force. On April 4, 2003, Smith personally manned a machine gun fully exposed to enemy fire near Baghdad International Airport. At the cost of his own life, he saved the lives of numerous wounded soldiers.[6]

Take Responsibility for Your Actions and Admit Your Mistakes

As a leader you will be taking responsibility for attaining an objective. The objective may be set by a higher level of your organization; it could be set by the people you lead; or it could be one that you set. Who sets the objective is unimportant. The size of the group isn't important either. It could be hundreds of thousands, or it could be you and one other person. Once you take on the leadership of a group, you and you alone are responsible for reaching the objective.

You can delegate to others the authority to do certain tasks that you lead, but there is no way that you can delegate responsibility. It doesn't make any difference whether those that follow you perform well or perform poorly, or even carry out your instructions. The responsibility remains yours.

You should of course take responsibility, and this includes admitting your mistakes. It's the right thing to do. In fact it is the only thing to do if you want to be a leader. Admit your mistakes, and those you lead will give you their trust and follow you anywhere. Fail to do this, and you will not be a leader for very long.

Martin L. Johnson tells the story of when, as an employee, he heard the CEO of Pioneer Hi-Bred International admit he had made a major mistake in the acquisition of another company, which cost Pioneer a lot of money. Right after selling the acquisition at a significant loss, he made the rounds of all his divisions and spoke to the employees: "I made a mistake buying Norand and I am sorry. I am sorry your profit-sharing was lower because of the purchase, and I am sorry your stock was hurt by the purchase. I will continue to take risks, but I am a bit smarter now, and I will work harder for you." Continued Johnson, "In the brief moment of silence before the questions started, I recall thinking that I would follow him into any battle."[7]

Praise in Public, Criticize in Private

No one likes to be told he did something wrong. We all like to think we do things right, even though we know this is not always true. When we do something really wrong, our feelings are even stronger. Even if no one else is there, the person who criticizes us must be careful; otherwise this criticism could cause us to react strongly against the critic.

Sometimes we must tell people we lead that they did something wrong. When we do this, we must first think, because criticism must always be done in a special way. I will show you what I am talking about shortly. If you really want to create enemies and make your job of leadership difficult, just tell people they did something wrong in front of others. You will embarrass the people you criticize. Not only will they not want to follow you; they may never forgive you. If others present happen to support those you have criticized, you may make even more enemies. Don't do it!

On the other hand, everyone likes praise. And when we receive praise, we'd like everyone to know about it. So the simple secret is, praise in public but criticize in private.

Both of these concepts are crucial. You must let people know how they are doing. You want them to know what they did that was wrong, so they won't do it again. But recognizing when someone does something right is equally important. And you want them to know what they did that was right, so they will do it again.

Kenneth Blanchard and Spencer Johnson, coauthors of *The One Minute Manager*, felt that the second element of this concept is so important that they gave it a special name. They called it "catching someone doing something right."[8]

See and Be Seen

I don't care whom you are leading; you can't lead from behind a desk. In the four months before the Allied invasion of Europe during World War II, General Eisenhower visited twenty-six divisions, twenty-four airfields, five warships, and numerous military bases, depots, hospitals, and many other military installations. All of his senior subordinates maintained similar visiting schedules. Eisenhower said, "There is among the mass of individuals who carry the rifles in war, a great amount of ingenuity and initiative. If men can naturally and without restraint talk to their officers, the products of their resourcefulness become available to all."[9]

Tom Peters, who has been a student of leadership since he served as a young naval officer in Vietnam, believes this too, because he found that seeing and being seen is done by effective leaders in every successful company and organization in and out of the military. Peters even popularized a technique called MBWA, or "management by wandering around," first developed by executives at Hewlett-Packard almost forty years ago.[10] When you go out and see—and are seen by—those you lead, you greatly increase the effectiveness of communications up and down the chain of command. You find out what's right and what's wrong in your organization. And you can correct things instantly. You can dramatize your ideas to your followers. That way the word gets around—fast.

General Patton on Visibility

As commander of the Third Army, General George S. Patton practiced MBWA. He found that his soldiers didn't always wear their heavy steel helmets. The helmet was an important factor for survival. More important was the implied lack of battlefield discipline, since helmets were required in combat by army regulations. Other things Patton saw also convinced him that discipline wasn't what it should be. Lack of discipline in combat cost lives and lost battles.

Patton took instant action to correct the situation. He issued orders that any soldier not wearing his steel helmet *and a tie* would be court-martialed.

Modern combat dress etiquette dictates that officers be indistinguishable from the soldiers they lead; otherwise, they may be singled out as targets by the enemy. However that conflicted with Patton's feelings about being visible to those he led. So Patton not only wore a helmet and tie; he fixed his jeep with flying flags. He wore a revolver on one hip and an automatic on the other. No one could mistake Patton on the battlefield, and his visits were legendary. His seeing and being seen helped make him a successful battlefield commander. It out-weighed the additional risk of being identified by the enemy.

Patton said, "The more senior the officer who appears with a very small unit at the front, the better the effect on the troops. . . . Corps and Army commanders must make it a point to be physically seen by as many individuals of their command as possible—certainly by all combat soldiers."[11]

Benefits of Visibility

By seeing and being seen, you can

- Know what's going on in your organization every day.
- Help those who need help.
- Get help from those who can supply help.
- Discover the real problems.
- Uncover opportunities you didn't know existed.
- Praise and recognize those that deserve it.
- Correct or discipline those that need it.
- Get your word out fast.
- Communicate your vision for the organization.
- Make sure everyone understands your goals and objectives.

Seeing and being seen sounds like a pretty simple action to take. It is. But with this simple action you will accomplish all of the above, and others will follow where you lead.

Make Striving a Game

Have you ever participated in a competitive sport? If not, I'm sure that you have at least watched one. Competitive sports include everything from golf to football, from boxing to gymnastics.

Competitive sports can be rough, fast, or slow; they require great skill, endurance, or knowledge. They can be played on the ground, above the ground, on ice, in water, or under water. They involve balls, rackets, carts, chariots, guns, cars, airplanes, boats, skis, skates, or ships. One ancient sport actually involved vaulting over live bulls.

Whatever the sport or the manner of its playing, all involve competition with one or more human beings. The competition makes the sport exciting and fun. Competitive sports are not work; they are play. While work tires us, we can play at competitive sports on and on. In this fact lies a secret which all of us can use to make our tasks fun rather than work. All you have to do is make striving a game. Not possible with your kind of task, you say? Let me assure you that it's possible with any task.

Records are set not on practice fields but in real competition such as the Olympic Games. The secret of setting records—and of peak performances—in anything in life resides in competition. At one time, educators concluded that competition brought too much pressure to bear in learning. A change was made: students no longer received letter grades; their only grades were pass or fail. Educators believed this would improve performance in the classroom and in real learning. The idea was that rather than "wasting time" competing, students would be learning. Instead, the exact opposite happened. Not only did students participate to a lesser extent in the classroom, but objective tests proved that students didn't learn as much.

Summary

Here are the specific actions to take if you want a followership:

- Make others feel important.
- Treat others as you would be treated yourself.

- Take responsibility for your actions and those of your group.
- Praise in public, criticize in private.
- Take the time to see and be seen.
- Use competition to make striving a game.

CHAPTER 18

• •

How to Develop Your Self-Confidence

• •

Around the end of the nineteenth century one of the wild gangs that roamed the old West took over a small Texas town. They shot up the bar, threatened the citizens, and drove the sheriff out of town. In desperation the town's mayor telegraphed the governor, pleading that he send a detachment of Texas Rangers to save the town. The governor agreed that the problem called for the famous Rangers, and promised that a detachment would be on the next day's train.

The following day the mayor himself met the train on which the Rangers were to arrive. Unbelievably, only one Ranger got off the train.

"Where are the rest of the Rangers?" asked the mayor.

"They aren't any more," was the answer.

"How can one Ranger handle the gang?" asked the mayor indignantly.

"Well, there's only one gang, ain't there?" replied the Ranger.

This story may not be 100 percent true, but it is based on fact. Fewer than a hundred Rangers protected the entire state of Texas. And no Ranger felt himself outnumbered, though he might be working alone. The Ranger would look the situation over and do what had to be done. He would organize and lead a posse, motivate disheartened citizens, and guide lawmen. The situation was almost always dangerous. Yet the Ranger routinely led and directed others in life-and-death situations. From such facts came legends like the story of the Ranger on the train, or the fictional hero you may have heard of. His creator called him "The Lone Ranger."

● ● ● ●

How is it possible that Heroic Leaders take charge and assume responsibility for lives, jobs, and billion-dollar companies? How is it possible that such leaders can accept almost inconceivable levels of responsibility for the future of nations, if not for mankind itself? How can it be that Heroic Leaders sometimes lead thousands or even millions of men and women successfully? Yet they may do all these things seemingly without blinking an eye. All of this comes from self-confidence. As a recent article proclaimed, "Self-confident people inspire confidence in others: Their audience, their peers, their bosses, their customers, and their friends. Gaining the confidence of others is one of the key ways in which a self-confident person finds success."[1] It is the secret that empowers Heroic Leaders. But where do they get such tremendous self-confidence?

Know You Can Succeed

An old Air Force training manual on leadership says, "No man can have self-confidence if not convinced in his own mind that he is qualified to perform the job he is assigned."[2] It's a fact. If you know that you can succeed at something, you will have self-confidence that you can do it. The truth is, it is impossible not to. So the problem is, how can you know you will succeed before you actually try something?

During the Cold War, General Curtis LeMay built the Strategic Air Command into the mightiest military force ever forged. Later he became Air Force chief of staff. Before World War II he was a thirty-year-old captain and a B-17 navigator responsible only for himself. Five years later he was a major general leading thousands. He was responsible not only for their lives and well-being but for the success of missions crucial to the outcome of the war.

As the old saying goes, nothing succeeds like success. This means that success breeds success, or that successful people tend to become more successful. In other words, if you have been successful in the past, you have a better chance of being successful in the future. But again, how can you become successful before you are successful? It's like the chicken and the egg. You can't have a chicken until you have an egg, but you can't have an egg until you have a chicken.

Fortunately, there is a way. You can have a little success before a big success. And a little success counts just as much as a big success as far as our belief system goes. This means that if you can win little victories in something, your psyche will believe that you can accomplish even greater things in the same area. Moreover, you will project this feeling outward, and others will begin treating you differently.

Champion bodybuilder and movie star Arnold Schwarzenegger, who became governor of California, described how his confidence began to develop while still in high school because of his taking up bodybuilding: "Before long people began looking at me as a special person. Partly this was the result of my own changing attitude about myself. I was growing, getting bigger, gaining confidence. I was given consideration I had never received before."[3]

Many leaders are trained this way. They acquire their self-confidence by leading successively larger organizations with greater responsibilities. At every step their belief grows that they can be successful. And that belief leads to the self-confidence necessary to do the job.

Four Ways to Build Self-Confidence and Leadership Skills

How do Heroic Leaders gain the self-confidence they need to lead others? How do Heroic Leaders acquire the belief in success necessary for the self-confidence to do the job? I'm going to give you four ways to build your self-confidence and develop your leadership skills. All Heroic Leaders have used these methods. If you adopt them, you will develop your self-confidence as a leader through numerous smaller successes. Every time you practice them, your belief in your own potential for success will be strengthened. In time, you will become a powerful leader. Moreover, you will be ready to assume major leadership responsibilities because you will have the necessary self-confidence.

1. Recognize That You Don't Need a Title

The first way to develop self-confidence while you develop your leadership skills is to become an uncrowned leader. You have hundreds of opportunities to become a leader if you want to. I promise that if you stop to look, you will find at least one opportunity, and probably more, every day. The truth is, people around you are positively crying for you to help them by seizing the opportunity to lead. You don't have to be a manager to be a leader. Being a manager has to do with doing things right. Being a leader has to do with doing the right things. You absolutely do not need to have an official position as a paid manager to be a leader.

How to Become an Uncrowned Leader

The first rule for becoming a successful uncrowned leader is to accept responsibility cheerfully on the job. Even more than accepting it, you must seek out leadership responsibility every chance you get.

Maybe there is a special report that needs to be done. Perhaps the boss is looking for someone to organize or coach your company's sports program. Does your office want to buy a new computer?

Who's going to handle the job of selecting and buying it? Do you have office parties or weekend get-togethers? Entertainment committee chairmanships are leadership positions also. Every organizing opportunity is another chance to be an uncrowned leader. And the more you look for and take on leadership roles, the easier it gets. Others will look more to you as their leader, and you will become more confident in your ability to lead.

How to Find Uncrowned Leadership Jobs

Your uncrowned leadership jobs don't need to be at work. Every day, immediate problems need to be solved, and people need a leader to help solve them. Look around and you will see that everyone is looking at everyone else to lead. No one seems to know what to do. Do you know what to do? Are you at least willing to try? If so, you will be instantly and automatically promoted to uncrowned leader. The strange thing is that in most cases you will discover that it is not that no one knows what to do. It is that no one wants to do the work or take responsibility for doing whatever needs to be done. Under these circumstances, you will be amazed at just how ready others are to follow your lead.

You Don't Need to Fight for Uncrowned Leadership

Please understand that you will also find yourself in situations where it seems everyone wants to lead. In some of these cases, people want to lead so badly they will actually fight one another to do so. You may or may not be able to help out here as the group's leader. In any case, you are unlikely to be asked. When you find yourself in this kind of situation, my advice is to sit back and stay out of the fight. If the situation is so critical that some action needs to be done, do it yourself. Help the group as best you can, but don't compete for leadership. No matter how terrific a leader you are, you won't lead in every situation you find yourself in. But that's not important: there are plenty of uncrowned leadership opportunities around.

2. Be an Unselfish Teacher and Helper

We succeed in life only to the extent that we help others succeed in their lives. That's true whether you are a Heroic Leader in combat or in the office or boardroom, or even an author of a book on leadership. If I am successful in helping you reach your goals as a leader, you will make me successful in my goals as an author. That's how life works.

To become a successful Heroic Leader, then, you must give up some of your time, some of your resources, and some of your self so that others can succeed. In doing so, you will develop your confidence and find success in uncrowned-leader jobs, without which you cannot move on to bigger leadership jobs.

3. Develop Your Expertise—in Something

Recall the rule that the leader must know his stuff in Chapter Two. Research has demonstrated conclusively that expertise is an important source of power which will automatically attract others to you and make you their uncrowned leader.

What is expertise? Expertise is in-depth knowledge or skill about some subject. It can be about marketing, flying, warfare, management, stocks, record keeping, investments, buying a car, getting a loan, bowling, or baseball. Your expertise can also be on what to eat, how to jog, or even the best way to mow your lawn. Expertise can be about anything human beings do.

Expertise and Leadership

Any expertise will cause people to seek you out as a leader. The frequency that people make you a leader because of your expertise depends on how relevant your expertise is to the people around you.

Let's say you have expertise as a bowler. Many people will seek you out and make you a leader—if you are in the company of other bowlers. If you want to be an uncrowned leader in a group that has few bowlers, don't depend on your bowling expertise.

If you have expert knowledge about how to do something that is important to the group, there isn't any question whether you'll be sought out as a leader. And with the increased opportunities to lead, you will continue to gain confidence.

Certainly one factor that led to George S. Patton's promotion to general just before World War II was his expertise with tanks. During World War I, Patton had been a full colonel by the age of only twenty-nine. He had led America's first tank unit in combat. When funds ran short and the Army had to cut back on tanks, Patton went back to the horse cavalry and returned to his permanent rank of captain. By 1940 he had worked his way back up to colonel. Then the Army needed someone with tank expertise. Patton was one of the few senior officers who had the needed expertise. The Army quickly made him a general.

Many "fast burners" in industry got to the top rapidly for the same reason. Think of Steven Spielberg, CEO of DreamWorks; Bill Gates, founder and CEO of Microsoft; Steve Jobs, who founded Apple; Mary Kay Ash, founder and CEO of Mary Kay Cosmetics; Frederick Smith, founder and chairman of Federal Express. They all shared a common attribute. They had expertise in something that was of importance to others.

If you want people to acknowledge you, even seek you out, as their unofficial leader, first develop a needed expertise.

Revealed: The Secret About Acquiring Expertise

There is a big secret about acquiring expertise. At least, not too many people seem to know it. You can become an expert in just about anything in only five years or less. There is only one requirement. You must put forth the effort.

Want proof? Steve Jobs and Steve Wozniak were college dropouts when they founded Apple Computers to become multimillionaires. But they had been building computers even in high school. The time it took them to become computer experts? About five years.

Do the Research to Convince Yourself

If you further doubt what I say about how long it takes to become an expert, I challenge you to do a little research. I want you to go to newspapers, magazines, and books and look up the careers of young men and women who are super-successful. I recommend that you look for young people; otherwise, you may be tempted to count total years of experience rather than only the years spent acquiring an expertise. For example, Colonel Harland Sanders was well past sixty when he began to market his secret family recipe, which eventually led to the multibillion-dollar Kentucky Fried Chicken franchise. You might figure that he had spent his entire life acquiring expertise in the fried chicken business. You would be wrong. He didn't begin to learn anything about fried chicken until he was sixty-two.

I suggest that you look at the careers of super-successful people who are young, not because older people can't become super-successful. Harland Sanders and Ray Kroc are just two examples among thousands. But if you look at younger successes, there will be no doubt about how long it took them to acquire the needed expertise. I'm not saying you will always find success within five years; sometimes success takes much longer. But we're not talking about success here. We're talking about expertise. If you want to be an expert at flying, karate, dancing, marketing, or business, you can do it. You can acquire the expertise you want, and it will take you five years or less. But don't forget: acquiring expertise is not automatic. You must put forth the effort required to do it. If you do, as Jobs, Wozniak, and hundreds of others did, you will gain the expertise, and people will seek you out as their leader.

4. Use Positive Mental Imagery

One of the most important exercises you can do to develop your confidence as a leader is to practice positive mental imagery. The effects of positive (and negative) imagery can best be illustrated by experimenting for yourself:

Imagine a two-by-four hardwood plank, twenty feet long, lying on the ground in front of you. If I put a $100 bill at one end and told you all you had to do was walk along the plank to keep it, you would have no trouble. You would stride confidently across and pick up the $100.

What if I raised the height of the plank to fifteen feet off the ground? You would probably still get to the $100, but it would be a lot more difficult. You would be much more careful where and how you stepped. Your stride would be much slower and more deliberate. What is the difference? The width and construction of the board hasn't changed in any way. Nor has the location of the prize relative to your starting position. Only the height has changed. And that shouldn't really make any difference, should it?

Now picture the plank suspended between two skyscrapers, several hundred feet up. Are you still ready to go for the $100? Would you insist on at least several thousand dollars or more to walk across the same twenty-foot plank? Even then, most people (who aren't professional tightrope walkers) would probably decide not to try it. If you did make the attempt, you would be mighty careful. Yet nothing has changed except the height. The real difference, of course, is the difference in mental images that the change in height creates. When the plank is on the ground, the $100 fills your mind. However, as the height increases, you focus less on the $100 and more on the chance of falling and the consequences of a fall.

Just as negative images can hurt your confidence as a leader, so too can positive images help your confidence, considerably. Chapter Five includes a number of stories about the power of expectation and picturing positive results. The most vivid account—and most relevant here—is that of psychologist Charles Garfield, the amateur weightlifter, who was able to increase his bench press by 30 percent (from 280 to 365 pounds!) with an hour's visualization practice.[4]

Summary

You can develop your self-confidence as a leader by taking four action steps. All have to do with the basic fact that your confidence increases as you accomplish leadership tasks successfully.

Do smaller and easier tasks first. Take on all that you can. Then progress to more difficult tasks. You will find them to be much easier than you thought.

Here are the four action steps to build your leadership confidence:

- Become an uncrowned leader by seeking out and volunteering to lead whenever you can. Others will come to you for leadership.

- Be an unselfish teacher and helper of others.

- Develop your expertise. Expertise is a source of leadership power.

- Use positive mental imagery. Mental simulations are rehearsals for success. They are interpreted by the mind as real experiences. They will boost your leadership confidence just like the actual experience.

CHAPTER 19

• •

How to Build a
Heroic Team

• •

In my seminars on leadership, I always ask this question: Can you think of any organization that has all of these attributes?

- The workers toil very hard physically, including weekends, with little complaint.
- The workers receive no money and little material compensation for their services.
- The work is dangerous, and workers are frequently injured on the job.
- The work is strictly voluntary.
- The workers usually have very high morale.
- The organization always has more applicants than can be employed.
- The workers are highly motivated to achieve the organization's goals.

Can there be such an organization on the face of the earth, or only in one's dreams? Before you come to a conclusion, consider the high school football team. It has all these qualities. True, a successful high school football star can go on to make megabucks as a professional player. However, the chance of that happening, considering the relative numbers of high school players and pro players, is very slim indeed. Few perform "work" on a football team for that reason.

I use football as an example, but you will find similar or even more amazing results in other sports. For years I have been fascinated with the story of Arthur Resnick, who coached a girls' soccer team in Scarsdale, New York. In a four-year period Coach Resnick's team won seventy-five consecutive matches. Of course it won the regional title every year. It actually took six years and 107 games before this team finally lost![1]

I know what you're thinking. This was one of those schools that train professional athletes. Every student was a jock. The male teams achieved even more dramatic results. All of these statements are 100 percent wrong. This was not a particularly athletic school. Other teams at the same school, both male and female, had only a mediocre record. Because of his incredible success, others have studied Coach Resnick's techniques. Stories about him and his team have appeared in magazines and newspapers including *Business Week*, the *Wall Street Journal*, and *Boardroom Reports*.

Why are business and management readers so interested in what the coach of a girls' soccer team did? Because they realize that if they can understand what Coach Resnick did to build his team, they can use the same techniques to build their own organizations.

Leadership and Athletics

Leadership on the athletic field correlates somewhat with leadership in other parts of life. After World War I the authorities at West Point decided to review the records of former cadets. They wanted to know whether anything in the records of cadets who later became general officers could have predicted their later success. Academically, there were no predictors. Some generals, such as MacArthur, had graduated first in their class. However, there were also generals who had graduated much lower in their class, like President Eisenhower. Some generals had been athletes; others had not. But it was a fact that a West Point graduate was more likely to become a general if he had been an athlete while a cadet. As a result of this research, athletics became required for all cadets.

General Douglas MacArthur's view is known to every West Point cadet. It is blazoned in stone on the main athletic building at West Point:

"On the fields of friendly strife are sown the seeds, that on other fields, on other days, will bear the fruits of victory."

Military leadership on the battlefield attempts to replicate athletic leadership on the playing field. Its many successes are demonstrated by elite military units as well as the sometimes incredible accomplishments and victories in combat against great odds by winning military teams. If you lead your organization or group like a winning football team, what an organization you can have! What accomplishments aren't possible, what victories can't be won? This is possible because you will have built a heroic team.

In this chapter I discuss how to apply the techniques used by every winning coach as well as every winning battlefield commander to build an unbeatable, heroic team.

What Every Winning Athletic Team Has

If you want to build an organization like a winning athletic team, begin by examining winning teams to see what makes them successful. Successful athletic teams have these characteristics:

Cohesion: Members stick together. They put the interests of the group over their own interests.

Teamwork: Members work together so as to maximize their individual strengths and minimize their weaknesses.

High Morale: Members have an inner feeling of well-being that is independent of external factors.

Esprit de Corps: Besides the members' individual sense of well-being, the organization as a unit shares high morale and confidence in its ability.

The rest of this chapter focuses on the first two characteristics, cohesion and teamwork. Chapter Twenty takes up the second pair, high morale and esprit de corps.

Cohesion

Cohesion is known in the military as a combat force multiplier. This means that the mere existence of strong cohesion in a unit can multiply its effectiveness in combat. Through strong cohesion, a smaller and weaker military force can overcome one that is larger and stronger.

Many units that fought in Vietnam lacked cohesion. This was due in part to the military's policy of rotating individual men stateside as they completed one year of combat duty. As a result there was little unit stability as replacements constantly arrived and veterans departed. American military organizations could have maintained the cohesion of these units by rotating the entire unit and replacing it with a new one. The policy of not doing this contributed to a decrease in unit motivation, discipline, and combat performance.[2] This lesson was not lost when the U.S. armed forces confronted Iraq in Operation Desert Shield and then went to war in Operation Desert Storm. For the most part, the individuals who went abroad with their units were the same ones who fought there. Even in these times of significant manpower shortage, the military tries to maintain unit integrity for those serving in Iraq and Afghanistan.

Boosting Performance

Cohesive organizations outperform organizations that lack cohesion again and again. One investigation discovered that when cohesion increased, soldiers' average performance scores in each of four major training areas were significantly better. Cohesion has this effect because good working relationships among the members of the group make for more efficient use of group assets. Such assets might include individual ability, available time, and assigned equipment. Also, in cohesive organizations the more talented voluntarily spent their free time teaching and coaching the less talented. Further, assuming high ability and high motivation, the more cohesion a group has, the better the group will perform.[3]

When an average athletic team that has played together for a while beats a group of all-stars who have not, this is usually the reason. Another study, which used computer simulation, analyzed competing business organizations. It found that organizational leadership was significantly associated with team cohesion, which in turn was significantly related to superior performance, underscoring the importance of developing strong group cohesion.[4]

Developing Strong Group Cohesion

If you want to develop strong cohesion in your organization, you must develop pride in membership. To feel pride, your group must feel they are in the best organization of its type, anywhere. If your organization is a production crew making automobile parts, each member must feel being part of the best production crew making automobile parts in that company, maybe in any company. The same principle applies across all kinds of business. Every one of your group members must regard the organization as the best of its kind.

If you are going to convince your group that they are the best, they are actually going to have to *be* the best in some relevant way. This is not as difficult as it may appear. The key is to focus on some element that is important to the group and to what you are trying to accomplish and to concentrate on being best at that.

You can do this right at the start, when you first become associated with your group. Assign tasks that you know members can perform well. As their skill and pride of accomplishment increase, select tasks that are progressively more difficult.

Of course, every time a task is completed successfully, make certain that the responsible individuals receive the recognition they deserve. And make sure your entire organization learns of every victory. Recognition comes in a variety of forms. Official letters of commendation are one way; however, even short handwritten notes, verbal praise, and a pat on the back, when earned, are appreciated.

Symbols Represent the Real Thing

You can and should encourage organizational mottoes, names, symbols, and slogans. They represent the real thing. That's why hearing the national anthem and seeing the flag waving can bring a lump to your throat and sometimes tears to your eyes. For Americans, it's not that the "Star-Spangled Banner" is such a beautiful tune. Originally, it was a beer-drinking song! Nor do the Stars and Stripes as a piece of art evoke emotion. Without the nation the flag represents, it is simply a multicolored piece of cloth. But representing what it does, it is extremely powerful, as are other symbols.

As a Heroic Leader, you should encourage such icons whenever you can, because they brand us for what we are—to ourselves and to others. And that's why the phrase "rally round the flag" is not empty in meaning.

Establishing Your Organization's Worth

Finally, you can improve group cohesion by establishing the worth of the organization and its values.[5] The more good things you can find and can say about your organization, the better. Everyone likes to be associated with winners and winning organizations. No one wants to be in an organization that is thought of as losing. If you can establish your group as a winner based on the organization's past, you are well on your way toward having a strong, cohesive unit. You can investigate and find good things in the history of your organization. What are your organization's traditions? What has your organization accomplished in the past that you can promote? The more you can find to promote, the better.

Note that I keep mentioning promotion. Once you ferret out this information about your organization, you've got to use it. You want everyone in your organization to know what a terrific organization they are associated with. Publicize this information in newsletters. Post it on bulletin boards; read the information at staff meetings. Use every technique you can to promote your organization as the best around. Get people excited about their membership in the group. Make them feel they are better than anyone else—in fact, the best.

One cautionary note: some leaders think they can promote their organization best by tearing down the reputation of the parent organization. This is a mistake. It will backfire. Not only will your superiors come down on you eventually; you will hurt the very cohesion you are trying to build. Again, no one wants to be associated with a losing organization, even if it is the parent organization. Even when things go wrong because of actions of the parent organization—and your organization has done its job—build support for both organizations, not one at the expense of the other.

If the members of your group feel that they are in the best organization of its type, which in turn is part of the best organization of its type, you will build a bonding force that is stronger than any glue. It is a cohesion that cannot be broken, and it will pay dividends in performance in any environment.

Teamwork

If you have watched successful athletic teams performing, you were probably amazed at how easy they made their plays look. So integrated was their performance that instead of seeing the individual members acting, you saw the team as a single entity in motion.

You may even have been seduced into thinking, "Say, that's not so hard. I can do that." If you participate in the same sport, or coach kids, you may have tried the same play of teamwork you saw performed by experts. Only then did you realize just how difficult it was for a group to pull off what you saw the well-coordinated team perform.

Accomplished teamwork may be seen not only in athletic events. In the military such performances happen daily on aircraft, ships, and tanks, in missile and artillery command centers, and in field training exercises. The performances are amazing. Not only does every team member seem to know exactly what to do, but they all know how to modify their individual performance to fit in with changes in the environment and minor changes in the performances of other members. The bottom line is that through teamwork the overall performance is greater than the sum of the performances of the individual team members.

Working Together

Peter Drucker found the same phenomenon in a well-run hospital. Doctors, nurses, X-ray technicians, pharmacologists, pathologists, and other health care practitioners all worked together to accomplish a single objective. Frequently he saw several people working on the same patient under emergency conditions. Seconds counted. Even a minor slip could prove fatal. Yet with a minimum amount of conscious command or control by any one individual, this medical team worked together toward a common end and followed a common plan of action under the overall direction of a doctor. The similarity to what you see on an athletic field would be striking.[6]

Teamwork in all activities is crucial. Years ago the Air Force did a study of their bomber crews in the Strategic Air Command. Individual performance improves with increased flying experience as measured by the number of flying hours. The researchers wanted to know how performance was affected by increased flying experience on a specific aircraft. They expected that more experience on a particular airplane would cause performance to improve. It did. However, the time a *crew* spent flying together was a far more accurate predictor of improved performance than individual flying experience.

Common Purpose

In any organization some groups and individuals are more glorified and recognized than others. Leaders should strive to build distinction in their own group, whether the work is developing high-technology products or digging ditches. However, as overall leader with responsibility for different groups, you must get the entire organization focused on a common purpose and provide recognition and some glory for all.

Part of General Patton's genius was his ability to get everyone focused on the common purpose by proving the importance of every individual in the organization. Read this excerpt from Patton's D-Day speech to his troops just prior to the landings at Normandy. You will see how Patton did it, and how you can do it, too.

> All of the real heroes are not storybook combat fighters, either. Every single man in this Army plays a vital role. Don't ever let up. Don't ever think that your job is unimportant. Every man has a job to do and he must do it. Every man is a vital link in the great chain.
>
> What if every truck driver suddenly decided that he didn't like the whine of those shells overhead, turned yellow, and jumped headlong into a ditch? The cowardly bastard could say, "Hell, they won't miss me, just one man in thousands." But, what if every man thought that way? Where in the hell would we be now? What would our country, our loved ones, our homes, even the world, be like?
>
> No, Goddamnit, Americans don't think like that. Every man does his job. Every man serves the whole.

Every department, every unit, is important in the vast scheme of this war.

The ordnance men are needed to supply the guns and machinery of war to keep us rolling. The Quartermaster is needed to bring up food and clothes because where we are going there isn't a hell of a lot to steal. Every last man on K.P. has a job to do, even the one who heats our water to keep us from getting the "G.I. Shits."

Each man must not think only of himself, but also of his buddy fighting beside him. We don't want yellow cowards in this Army. . . .

One of the bravest men that I ever saw was a fellow on top of a telegraph pole in the midst of a furious fire fight in Tunisia. I stopped and asked what the hell he was doing up there at a time like that. He answered, "Fixing the wire, Sir." I asked, "Isn't that a little unhealthy right about now?" He answered, "Yes Sir, but the Goddamned wire has to be fixed." I asked, "Don't those planes strafing the road bother you?" And he answered, "No, Sir, but you sure as hell do!" Now, there was a real man. A real soldier. There was a man who devoted all he had to his duty, no matter how seemingly insignificant his duty might appear at the time, no matter how great the odds.

And you should have seen those trucks on the road to Tunisia. Those drivers were magnificent. All day and all night they rolled over those son-of-a-bitching roads, never stopping, never faltering from their course, with shells bursting all around them all of the time. We got through on good old American guts. Many of those men drove for over forty consecutive hours. These men weren't combat men, but they were soldiers with a job to do. They did it, and in one hell of a way they did it. They were part of a team. Without team effort, without them, the fight would have been lost. All of the links in the chain pulled together and the chain became unbreakable.[7]

Patton's language may have been more profane than many of us would appreciate. Others might have said it differently, without the profanity, but with equal effectiveness. But that was Patton. He was speaking to soldiers, and that was his style. What I want you to notice is how he brought every individual in his Army into one big team in his speech, working together for a common purpose.

Developing Teamwork Off the Job
There is another way you can develop teamwork in your organization. That is to encourage your members to participate in sports together outside of work. You should participate yourself. If it is a sport that you are particularly skilled in, well and good. If not, that's all right too. The important thing is to play with the members of your organization.

These don't need to be contact sports—and maybe they shouldn't. Try to select a sport that everyone can participate in, male or female, in great shape or not. Playing together will help your "team" develop the teamwork that will spill over into other areas of your lives. And that is what you are after.

Summary

These are your first actions in building your organization like a winning team:

- Develop group cohesion.
- Develop teamwork.

Now turn to Chapter Twenty to look at two other important concepts for building your organization like an athletic team: high morale and esprit de corps.

CHAPTER 20

• •

How to Build High Morale and Esprit de Corps

• •

Winning athletic teams have two other important character-istics, which usually go together: morale and esprit de corps. Every winning athletic team has them. Think of high morale as a sense of well-being or exaltation felt by an individual member of a group. Esprit de corps is a collective or group feeling of exaltation or of being unstoppable. You want both to build a heroic team. This chapter discusses ways to do exactly that.

High Morale

The biggest difference between the team member who works for an ordinary leader and one who works for a Heroic Leader is that the first looks forward to the weekend, and the second to the work-week. What a difference! When your workers have high morale, they too will begin to look forward to the week rather than the weekend. People with high morale have fun. Naturally, they look forward to having fun and feeling good. That this will happen during the workweek is good for you. That there are five days of fun and feeling good versus only two on the weekend is good for them. It's a double win.

How can you achieve this? How can you attain such high morale among your workers that they would rather be on the job than doing other things? And how long will it take? You may have heard that it takes months or even years to build high morale, but this is simply untrue. General George S. Patton said, "In a week's time, I can spur any outfit into a high state of morale."[1] Here's how to do it.

Cutting Others In

If you want your group to have high morale, you must let them in on the action. By this I mean that your workers must share ownership with you in accomplishing any project or task. One of the greatest management experts of all time was a man by the name of Chester Barnard. Barnard learned his management the hard way. He worked himself up from the bottom at AT&T to head up the company. Then, in the late 1930s, he wrote *The Functions of the Executive*, which is still widely read. His conclusions are worth studying. Said Barnard, "Scarcely a man, I think, who has felt the annihilation of his personality in some organized system, has not also felt that the same system belonged to him because of his own free will he chose to make it so."[2]

When you give your people ownership, they feel much differently toward the task than if you set yourself as the only one responsible. The difference is between being an important team member and an organizational cog. When people have ownership, they are under the influence of feelings of an entirely different type.

This is quite evident in some of the things we've begun to do in Iraq, including a unique law enforcement training program taught with Americans and coalition advisers but by Iraqis. Moreover, trainees are also part of the process that ensures the best training possible. Trainees participate in their own training, correcting each other in proper weapon positioning or in maneuvers through a building to neutralize threats from mock terrorists. According to advisers, the collaborative learning environment results in high esprit de corps among the trainees. However, the ownership also results in high morale. This is evident by the spontaneous clapping and cheering that erupts when a student team quickly and efficiently moves through a drill.[3]

Staying Alert

If you want high morale in your organization, you must constantly monitor what is going on. Keep your eyes and ears open, look for trends, and most important get around to visit and talk with people in your organization every day. That way you'll not only know how your people feel; you'll also be aware of everything that is going on.

If the people in your organization become down-hearted or begin to show the negative effects of defeat or flagging morale, you should know about it, and take quick action to do something about it. Sometimes a simple joke can turn things around. Other times you may need to do more. The important principle is to know what's going on in your organization and then take timely action to influence it. That way you will have a major impact on events rather than the other way around.

Esprit de Corps

After World War I, General James Harbord, a senior Army leader, commented on his experiences in France. "Discipline and morale influence the inarticulate vote that is constantly taken by masses of men when the order comes to move forward—a variant of the crowd psychology that inclines it to follow a leader," he said. "But the Army does not move forward until the motion has carried. 'Unanimous consent' only follows cooperation between the individual men in ranks."[4] In other words, there is a group spirit (esprit de corps) which you must reach in order to motivate groups of people to do things, even in the military and despite the influence of orders. How do you develop esprit de corps? For my money, esprit de corps is built on three things: your personal integrity as leader, mutual confidence, and a focus on contribution rather than personal gain.

Maintaining Integrity

Chapter One made absolute integrity the first of the eight laws of leadership. Actually, integrity is involved in all of your actions as a leader. I do not believe you can develop esprit de corps without it. Thomas E. Cronin, a political scientist and writer who was also a White House Fellow, confirms that integrity "is perhaps the most central of leadership qualities."[5]

Major General Perry M. Smith tells a story about Babe Zaharias in his book *Taking Charge*. Babe Zaharias was a champion sportswoman in the 1932 Olympics. Later, as a professional golfer, she penalized herself two strokes after the round she was playing was over. The penalty strokes cost her first place in a major tournament. Why did she do it? It turns out that she accidentally played the wrong ball. A friend later asked her why she penalized herself. "After all, Babe," said the friend, "no one saw you. No one would have known the difference." "I would have known," replied the great Babe.[6]

If you want to build esprit de corps, you must demonstrate integrity like Babe Zaharias. If you do, it won't be long before everyone in your organization knows that you can be trusted, that you say what you mean and mean what you say. The members of your organization will return the favor. They will demonstrate integrity in dealing with you, and with each other, and the esprit de corps in your organization will soar.

Rear Admiral Dave Oliver Jr. is a former submarine captain who practiced and studied leadership at great length, and then wrote a book about it. Admiral Oliver had this to say about integrity:

"In many large organizations there is a contingent of thought that the contest usually goes to the man willing to sail closest to the fine line drawn between truth and less-than-that. Some self-styled pragmatists regale audiences with stories that might lead a novice to believe that success is the province of only the most gnarled and least scrupulous bureaucratic battlers. That has not been my experience."[7]

Showing Real Concern for Your People

The *Armed Forces Officer* says that esprit de corps is "the product of a thriving mutual confidence between the leader and the led, founded on the faith that together they possess a superior quality and capability." If you want to build mutual confidence, I have found that you must demonstrate your real concern for the welfare of those for whom you are responsible.

Demonstrating your real concern gets back to the priorities you must have as a leader. First comes your mission or organizational goals. Then comes the welfare of your people. If you are a real leader, your personal interests come dead last. Those who follow you will accept hardships, put up with your personal mistakes and idiosyncrasies, and even willingly risk their lives—under certain conditions. First and foremost, the cause must be worthwhile. Then you must demonstrate the proper priority of interests.

When I first started university teaching, I asked my friend, then department chairman Marshall E. Reddick, how he got such high ratings from his students on his teaching evaluations. "It's easy," he said. "Students will do whatever you ask, even the most difficult assignments, so long as they realize it is to their benefit, and not yours." Here was a near perfect example of applying the priorities of a leader to the classroom. First came the teacher's responsibility to impart knowledge. And then, combined with this, Marshall taught in such a way that it was to the students' benefit. Marshall's own interests came last.

George Patton was a tough general to work for. He drove his men mercilessly. Patton also made lots of mistakes. You may have heard about the incident when Patton slapped and berated a soldier who was suffering from combat psychosis. Patton also gave a speech in which he used profanity to a group of mothers whose sons had been killed in the war. In a postwar comment, he seemed to equate Nazis with Republicans and Democrats. These mistakes caused Eisenhower to fire this four-star warrior twice, despite his tremendous abilities and successes.

You may have heard about these mistakes, or seen them depicted by George C. Scott when he played Patton in the award-winning movie about his life. But did you also know that Patton had one of the lowest combat casualty rates of any commander during World War II?

Even as a twenty-nine-year-old colonel during World War I, Patton demonstrated real concern for the lives of his men. On being given command of the first American tank unit by General Pershing, he said, "Sir, I accept my new command with particular enthusiasm because with the eight tanks, I believe I can inflict the greatest number of casualties on the enemy with the smallest expenditure of American life."[8]

Patton repeatedly demonstrated a very real concern for his men despite his toughness. Because Patton demonstrated this concern, and had his priorities right, he and his men developed a high mutual confidence, which led to an unbeatable esprit de corps. As a result, his men loved him despite his foibles. And they were victorious.

Focusing on Contribution

When John F. Kennedy was sworn in as president of the United States, he exhorted his countrymen, "Ask not what your country can do for you. Ask instead, what you can do for your country." Kennedy knew how to get people to focus on the right objective. He pointed out that we could do great things together if people focused on what they could contribute rather than on what they could get. President Kennedy was assassinated before most of his goals could be reached. But the esprit de corps which he cultivated in the country continued long after him. Through that spirit, Americans inaugurated civil rights legislation, which revolutionized the country; made the first lunar landing; and successfully kept Russian missiles out of Cuba.

A switch from gain to contribution is easier than you might think. All of us play one of two games whenever we do anything. One game is "Get All You Can." The other is "Give All You Can." Regardless of which game is played, all play to win. You can bet that a group whose members are playing "Get All You Can" has little or no esprit de corps. On the other hand, you can actually feel the positive spirit in a group whose members are playing "Give All You Can."

Which game is your organization playing? If people are playing "Get All You Can," you've got to turn them around fast. If you don't, your organization will enjoy little esprit de corps and perform marginally at best. To get your group to play "Give All You Can," you must take positive actions. You must tell them the game, show them the game, and keep score in the game. To get started, decide where you want your organization to go. Then, over time, build a consensus for your goals by explaining them and getting input from your group's members. Develop and promote a plan of action and make assignments along with milestone dates.

Once you begin, everything that can go wrong will. You will encounter what Clausewitz called "battle friction." There will be setbacks, discouragement, and defeats. You must positively carry on. You must encourage—and demand—continued contribution and further sacrifice even in the face of adversity. Simultaneously, you must keep score in "Give All You Can." That means rewarding major contributors and sometimes punishing those who are still playing the old game. This is not always easy. Some who contributed nothing during "Get All You Can" continue to play that game. Frequently, they have to be brought around to understand the new game. All the time, you must set the example of being the number-one contributor. You need to do this without compromise, because you won't fool your organization. Not for a minute. The first time you begin playing "Get All You Can," you can expect your organization to follow your lead the same day.

Once you know that the members of your organization are focused on contributing to its benefit over their own, you won't need to wonder whether your organization has a high esprit de corps. You will see it with your own eyes and hear it as people tell you how happy they are to be in your organization.

Arthur Ochs Sulzberger Sr. is chairman emeritus of The New York Times Company. He is also a former Marine Corps captain. About his experiences in running the *New York Times* he said, "I quickly learned that team work—all pulling together toward an identifiable common goal—worked far better than rushing head-long 'over the top' only to discover that no one was behind you."[9]

Summary

This chapter completes the roster of elements needed to build a winning organization that looks like a winning football team. You'll have a heroic organizational team that can compete with the pros and win, even under the most difficult circumstances, if you apply these four elements:

- Cohesion
- Teamwork
- High morale
- Esprit de corps

CHAPTER 21

. . . .

How to Motivate When Times Get Tough

. . . .

There is little question that it is easier to motivate others when conditions are overwhelming. Those are tough times. But consider this—if you can motivate others under the worse conditions, you can motivate under just about any conditions. So it's a subject well worthwhile looking at. When times get tough, what motivates people to do things for you or for your organization? The truth is that no one single factor motivates all your people all the time. Different people are motivated by different things at any one point. But a big mistake that leaders make regarding motivation is not understanding what motivates most of their followers most of the time. And the worst mistake is thinking that those who follow you are motivated primarily by one thing when in fact they are motivated by something entirely different.

What Matters Most

Social scientists have studied many industries to determine what factors employees consider most important in their jobs. The results have been known for some time; they are not secret. One study was done by the Public Agenda Foundation and noted by John Naisbitt and Patricia Auberdene in their book *Re-inventing the Corporation*. They found that "Work with people who treat me with respect," "Interesting work," and "Recognition for good work" topped the list. Far down were "job security," "high pay," and "good benefits."[1] Almost twenty years later a similar survey was conducted. Guess what? Same results.[2] And my psychologist wife tells me that over the years similar questionnaires have been given to hundreds of thousands of employees with very similar results.

Ninety percent of the leaders I survey in my seminars put one or more of the bottom-ranked trio—job security, high pay, and good benefits—in the top-five motivators. That is, they thought these factors were what mattered most to their employees. But these three factors are usually far down on the list.

This doesn't mean that job security, high pay, and good benefits aren't important. They are. In times of economic crisis, you can bet they will be the top three listed. But with few exceptions, other factors are more frequently cited as more important motivators.

I found more evidence years ago when I worked as an executive recruiter. It was my job to find top executives for my client companies according to detailed job specifications we prepared together. Usually the candidates for these positions were already employed in high positions at other companies. A good part of the job was convincing these high-flying executives that it was worth their time to look at a new opportunity.

Yes, compensation, benefits, and security played a part in their decisions. But even when offered compensation increases of 30 percent or more, many executives just weren't interested. For those that were interested, the increased salary and benefits were usually more meaningful as signals that the new job was more important and therefore a better opportunity. And some executives left their positions for jobs with lower salaries, fewer benefits, and less security. This was either because the new position presented a greater opportunity to them in other ways, or because they were dissatisfied in their present position despite the higher pay and benefits.

Drucker's Volunteer Paradigm

Peter Drucker spent the last fifteen to twenty years of his life focused on nonprofit organizations. Many of the organizations he worked with contained more volunteers than paid employees. From his experience with these organizations and their members, he formulated an interesting concept: fulltime employees must be managed as if they were volunteers. His reasoning was that the workplace, even in nonvolunteer corporations, had changed to such an extent that a complete makeover in how workers were treated and motivated was in order. He noted that although full-time employees were paid, pay was no longer the main issue except under extreme economic circumstances.

"We have known for fifty years that money alone does not motivate to perform," he wrote. This was true because unlike their predecessors, modern knowledge workers had mobility; they could leave one firm and go somewhere else with relative ease. Moreover, they had their own means of production, that is, their knowledge. From these facts he concluded that what motivates volunteers, who do not get a paycheck, is what should also be used to motivate regular fulltime employees.[3]

What People Want on the Job

In the upper half of the list of top motivators, the following factors had the highest impact on motivation:

- Working with people who treat me with respect
- Interesting work
- Recognition for good work

- Chance to develop skills
- Working for people who listen if you have ideas about how to do things better
- A chance to think for myself rather than just carry out instructions

What do these factors all have in common? For one thing, none of them will cost you very much to implement compared with pay, benefits, or providing perfect job security. For another, these are factors you can improve regardless of limitations on salary or benefits placed by your parent organization.

Think about what this means to you as a leader who wants to motivate people to higher levels of performance. You can probably improve today most of these factors considered important by employees, and the effort will probably cost very little.

Respect

Isn't it within your power to treat people with respect and make sure that others who work for you do the same? Certainly every human being deserves to be treated with respect. Many outstanding leaders maintain that you should treat those who work for you with more than respect, and they have proved it by doing so.

The night before the Battle of Austerlitz, Napoleon went from campfire to campfire in his army. At every stop men gathered around him. Napoleon joked with his men and thanked them for their loyalty. He assured them of victory and explained how he had arranged for medical aid to come to them as swiftly as possible if they were wounded.[4]

Do you think Napoleon treated his men with respect, even more than respect? He surely did, and you can bet this respect was returned as well.

> "Promise us," shouted a veteran grenadier, "that you will keep yourself out of the fire."

"I will do so," Napoleon answered; "I shall be with the reserve until you need me."[5]

James MacGregor Burns, an American political scientist, wrote an outstanding scholarly book called simply *Leadership*.[6] In fact the book was so outstanding that it won the Pulitzer Prize. His succinct advice: "In real life, the most practical advice for leaders is not to treat pawns like pawns, nor princes like princes, but all persons like persons."[7]

Interest

Can you provide interesting work, or can you make the work your people must do interesting in some way? There are many opportunities to do this if you think about it. And this is why bringing in an element of competition can increase the productivity of your organization.

The importance of *interest* in fostering motivation is not a brand-new concept. Almost a hundred years ago Professor Warren Hilton wrote: "It is not enough to have a mere general passion for success. Mere indefinite wishing for success will never get you anywhere. Besides this general passion, you must have definite interests continually renewed. You must give the mind something specific and tangible and immediate to work upon. You must incessantly add new details. Otherwise interest, attention, and activity will wane. Your biggest problem is how to keep your efficient output of mental energy at a high level. The solution lies in maintaining interest."[8]

Recognition for Good Work

How many ways can you think of right now to recognize good work? How many different awards and rewards could you give to those who work for you to acknowledge their accomplishments? What could you do to publicize your followers' successes? How many ways can you say, "Congratulations, we're proud of you"?

Everyone wants recognition. Connie Podesta and Jean Gatz, management consultants and authors of *How to Be the Person Successful Companies Fight to Keep*, quote one CEO who confided his frustration and distress: "I have worked so hard to turn this company around. I have managed to keep our profits up without laying off one person. I provide excellent benefits, and I'm willing to pay for my employees to go to school. I spend a great deal of money on picnics, parties, and celebrations because I want them to enjoy their jobs and feel as though this is a family they can count on. Very few of them have ever said thank you or even seem to appreciate how hard I try to make this a great place to work. On the other hand, if one little thing goes wrong or I have to say no to any of their ideas, some of them threaten to quit. And others won't speak to me."[9]

"Tough," you say. "The guy has to learn to be more thick-skinned." "If he can't take the heat, he should stay out of the kitchen!" That's all very true. But here is someone who has made it to the top of a company. He's making good money and has power and responsibility. Yet even he craves recognition. If this is true of a person in a position of considerable power, think how true it must be for everyone else—including everyone who would follow you.

There are many ways to recognize your employees. Management expert Bob Nelson actually identified over a thousand! He published them in a book, *1001 Ways to Reward Employees*.[10]

Opportunities to Develop Skills

Do you create the opportunity for those in your organization to develop their skills? Can you provide special courses in-house? How about a few hours off every week to complete a college degree? Could you perhaps hire a physical fitness or yoga instructor to work with employees during lunch or after work? Sometimes one of your employees has an ability or unique knowledge and

would be willing to impart it to other employees. All you need
to do is ask. And please don't forget the requirement for you and
other leaders in your organization to act as teachers. Of course,
by teaching you also learn. To quote the New Testament, "Thou
therefore which teaches another, teaches thou not thyself?"
(Romans 2:21).

A Receptive Ear

There is little question that listening motivates. It may be far
more important in leadership than you ever realized. Some time
ago I had the opportunity to talk about top-level military leadership with seven four-star generals and admirals. These were
individuals who had reached the very top of their profession
before retiring. They had been chiefs of staff of their services,
commanders in chief, and in one case chairman of the Joint
Chiefs of Staff. One of the very few factors which set them apart
from other highly qualified combat leaders (who did not reach
the top) was their ability to listen. In one way or another, every
one of them mentioned this as an important, if not critical factor
in leadership.

General Bernard P. Randolph was the commander of Air
Force Systems Command. Before the Cold War ended and this
command disappeared, to be replaced by Air Force Materiel
Command, this organization did all of the Air Force's research
and development work, which included all of its advanced airplanes, missiles, satellites, and "Star Wars"—everything. In
addition to commanding an organization that was crucial to
the nation's defense, General Randolph was only the second
African-American Air Force officer to earn four stars, and he
was also the only navigator to ever achieve this rank. When
asked in an interview to explain his leadership philosophy,
he answered, "Ask your people what's important to them, and
listen."[11]

When Robert W. Galvin was chairman of the board and CEO of Motorola, his company was doing $1.5 billion in annual sales and employing fifty thousand people around the globe. What did the head of this leviathan company emphasize in his leadership practices? "I emphasize listening," said Galvin. "We strive to hear what other people want us to hear, even though they don't always come out and say it directly."[12]

McCormick, the specialty food company, exceeded $3 billion in annual sales in 2008, almost double 1998 sales.[13] McCormick has earned an international reputation as a company that knows how to listen to its people and integrate even lower-level employees into decision making. It calls itself "The World's Largest Spice Company." Then-chairman and president Harry K. Wells explained the company's success in these words: "Because of an underlying attitude that the company has developed over the years about how people interact, we have an atmosphere that allows anyone here to sit down and have meaningful dialogues about our policies and our objectives for the future."[14]

A Chance to Think for Themselves

Are you open to letting your people think for themselves? Just tell people *what* to do, and let them decide how to do it for themselves. This doesn't mean that you shouldn't give help if asked, only that people have their own brains, experience, and unique backgrounds. That's why they are assigned to their duties and not you—and why they're such valuable commodities.

You can't do all of the thinking for everyone in your organization. Even if you could, you would be ill-advised to do so. If all your people thought exactly like you, your organization would have a pretty limited source of ideas. Perhaps even more important is researchers' discovery that the effect of many brains working together is greater than the sum of the effects considered separately. If you try to do all the thinking in your organization yourself, you lose this vital synergy.

Let those you lead do their own thinking and you'll be amazed at what they come up with and how they use their expertise to solve your problems.

When Salary, Job Security, and Benefits Do Matter

Salary, job security, and good benefits are important, but they are not of primary importance. You may say, "Listen, in my company people work primarily for the pay and benefits, and that's it." But think again.

If you've been in a company for any length of time, you've seen people leave voluntarily. When asked why they are leaving, they will almost invariably respond that they have better offers else-where. They may then begin to detail all the advantages of their new positions: higher salaries, bigger jobs, more benefits, bigger offices, and so on.

If you listen carefully, however, you'll hear another message, even if it isn't verbalized. The message is this: "These people who hired me really appreciate what I have to offer. They recognize my real importance to a much greater extent than happens here. They are giving me all these benefits because I am especially important." In other words, although the higher salary and additional benefits were inducements to leave an organization, they may only provide the rationale, not the real reason.

Recall again that in many organizations pay, benefits, and job security are nonexistent. Yet those who work in these orga-nizations may perform to their maximum. Remember the sports teams in Chapter Nineteen? There are also voluntary hospital workers and those who for low pay work on dangerous archeo-logical digs, for the Peace Corps, the Big Brother programs, the Boy Scouts and Girl Scouts, and hundreds of other organiza-tions. What part do salary, benefits, and security play in their motivation?

Summary

You can take specific steps to motivate those you lead:

- Work on the most important factors first. High salary, good benefits, or job security are more frequently of lesser importance than you may think.
- Treat those you lead with respect—always.
- Make the work interesting.
- Always give recognition for good work.
- Give those you lead a chance to develop their skills.

CHAPTER 22

How to Take Charge in Crisis Situations

When Lieutenant General Bernard L. Montgomery took charge of the British Eighth Army in Africa during World War II, he faced major problems. The Eighth Army had been defeated by the German general Rommel and his Afrika Korps. After finally winning a victory, Montgomery's predecessor, General Auchinleck, had been persuaded to attack again prematurely. He was defeated. An immediate counterattack by Rommel was feared. The Eighth Army had made withdrawal after withdrawal over the months; now orders were out to prepare for yet another withdrawal. Morale in the Eighth Army was at an all-time low when Montgomery arrived.

Here's what Montgomery did immediately:

- He canceled all previous orders about withdrawal.

- He issued orders that in the event of enemy attack there would be no withdrawal. The Eighth Army would fight on the ground they held. In Montgomery's words, "If we couldn't stay there alive, we would stay there dead."

- He appointed a new chief of staff.

- He formed a new armored corps from "various bits and pieces."

- He changed the basic fighting units from brigade groups and ad hoc columns to full divisions.

- He initiated plans for an offensive, saying, "Our mandate is to destroy Rommel and his Army, and it will be done as soon as we are ready."

Speaking later of the events of his first day in charge, he said, "By the time I went to bed that night, I was tired. But I knew that we were on the way to success."[1]

Only a few months later, Montgomery's Eighth Army attacked at El Alamein and won a major victory. It was the turning point of the war in the North African theater of operations. It also helped gain for Montgomery a promotion to field marshal. That's the British equivalent of full general in the U.S. Army. The victory also won for him the title "Montgomery of Alamein."

Establish Your Objective

In Chapter Three, I talked about the need for vision. Vision is necessary for leadership under all circumstances. You can't get there until you know where "there" is. Without vision, you have no "there," no objective.

When Montgomery was given command of the British Eighth Army, he wasn't just told, "Here's your Army—see what you can do with it." He was given a definite objective by his boss, Field Marshal Alexander: "My orders from Alexander were quite simple; they were to destroy Rommel and his Army."[2]

Montgomery believed that having a clear objective was critical. "I hold the view that the leader must know what he himself wants. He must see his objective clearly and then strive to attain it; he must let everyone else know what he wants and what are the basic fundamentals of his policy. He must, in fact, give firm guidance and a clear lead."[3]

Communicate Your Objective

General Patton was a real believer in communication, so much so that in training he kept a microphone constantly nearby. Porter B. Williamson, one his officers during this period, reports:

> Our desert radio broadcasting station had one unusual feature. There was a microphone in Gen. Patton's office and a second microphone was by his bed in his tent. Day and night Gen. Patton could cut off all broadcasting and announce a special message or order from his personal mike. When the music would click off we knew we would hear, 'This is Gen. Patton.'
>
> Often Gen. Patton would say, 'I want every man to be alert tomorrow because we are doing the maneuvers for a lot of brass from Washington who don't know the first thing about tanks or desert warfare. We must show them how wars can be won with speed. I am counting on every man.'[4]

General Patton also believed in answering his own phone. In his book *War As I Knew It*, he says, "In my opinion, generals—or at least the Commanding General—should answer their own telephones in daytime. This is not particularly wearisome because few people call a general, except in emergencies, and then they like to get him at once."[5]

General Patton knew the importance of communication in taking charge, and he spared nothing to ensure that he could communicate with those he led. And he wasn't the only one to use this technique. Norm Lieberman was the project manager working for North American Aviation and was in charge of the development of the F-100 in the late 1950s. He used the same technique as Patton's. A public address system was set up in the factory. From his office he could communicate with his engineers and workmen instantly and effectively. It seems the F-100 was completed without cost overruns and in minimum time. This rarely happens. The Air Force thought quite highly of the airplane as well. Perhaps today's aerospace leaders should use this technique more often.

Be Bold

Patton was certainly a Heroic Leader. Known as "Old Blood and Guts," he was bold. He knew how to deal with crisis. Patton's boldness was with a definite purpose. He said, "In planning any operation, it is vital to remember, and constantly repeat to oneself, two things: 'In war nothing is impossible, provided you use audacity.' If these two principles are adhered to, with American troops victory is certain."[6]

Konosuke Matsushita was one of the central figures in the Japanese economic miracle after World War II. The year Matsushita died, the revenues of his company, Matsushita Electric, were $42 billion. That sum exceeded the sales of Bethlehem Steel, Colgate-Palmolive, Gillette, Goodrich, Kellogg, Olivetti, Scott Paper, and Whirlpool, combined. On one occasion, when one of Matsushita's divisions was losing money, Matsushita was immediately on the scene. As reported by Harvard professor John Kotter, this is how the conversation went:

> "I could understand if sales were zero and the deficit was in personnel costs," Matsushita yelled, "but you've got sales of one hundred billion yen and are nine billion in the red. Responsibility for running this mess lies with you and the executives under you. The head office must

also take responsibility because they recently lent you that twenty billion yen. Tomorrow, I'm going to talk to them about getting it back."

"But Mr. Matsushita, that would mean disaster for us! It's five days to payday. At the end of the month we will owe money for materials and parts. If you take that twenty billion yen back now, we won't be able to pay for them."

"That's right, but I'm not going to lend you any money if you and your colleagues are going to run an operation like this. I'm pulling your loan tomorrow."

"But then we'll go bankrupt!"

"You've got four thousand superb employees working here. Talk it over with them, get their ideas, and come up with a reconstruction plan that will work. If you can get a plan like that together, I'll write a letter of recommendation to Sumitomo Bank for you. With that letter, they're sure to give you a twenty billion yen loan using the land, buildings, and equipment here as collateral. Now, get to work!"[7]

Sometimes boldness requires strong medicine. The Heroic Leader knows how to dispense it.

Be Decisive

People do not like to follow leaders who cannot make up their minds or have trouble coming to a decision. To take charge means coming to a decision and communicating it.

In July 1863, General George Gordon Meade defeated Robert E. Lee at the Battle of Gettysburg. But because he was indecisive about pursuing Lee, Lee's Army of Northern Virginia was able to retreat across the Potomac River without further harm. If General Meade had pursued Lee immediately, he could have cut the Army of

Northern Virginia off before it crossed the Potomac. Lee's army could have been defeated and the war ended that year. Instead, because Lee was allowed to escape, the Civil War went on for another two years with tens of thousands of casualties.

Maybe you have trouble coming to a decision because you don't have all the facts; however, you will never have all the facts. That's the nature of leadership. Almost all the time you must make decisions without knowing everything that might help you make a decision.

It is true that the longer you wait, the more facts you will have. Sometimes it is necessary to wait for important facts before making a decision. But you must weigh the gain in information against the negative impact of delay. Elements of the situation can change; an opportunity may be lost; your competition may beat you to the market. Those who follow you will at best be uncomfortable at not having a decision. If you make indecisiveness a habit, they will not want to follow you.

Some leaders tell themselves they are putting off a decision to get more facts. Although, again, at times more facts are necessary, frequently these leaders are simply afraid to make a decision. Failing to make a decision is also a decision. It is a decision to leave everything to chance or the initiative of others. It is certainly not a sign of a take-charge leader—and usually it results in failure.

To be a Heroic Leader, follow the recommendation of W. Clement Stone, the self-made billionaire. Stone said that when you feel yourself putting off anything without reason, say these three words out loud: "Do it now!"

Dominate the Situation

As a leader in circumstances where you must take charge, you must dominate the situation, or it will dominate you. This means you must take positive action to gain control, and you must continue to initiate action to maintain control. If you fail to do this, you will spend your time and energy continually responding to the actions of others or to crises of your environment, a pattern called *firefighting*. Firefighting will steal your time, leaving no time for you to take charge with new initiatives.

There are two reasons for this, and they aren't complicated. Within any take-charge situation lies a desperate need for Heroic Leadership. If you do not take the initiative, someone else must fill the leadership vacuum and will attempt to take charge. You may be the formal leader, and the other person may not be as experienced, as qualified, or as trained as you—but it makes no difference. If you fail to take the initiative, someone else will attempt to, and you will have to fight to regain the leadership role.

The second reason you must dominate the situation immediately has to do with your environment. If you fail to take the initiative, the environment tends to become even worse. First you had one problem; now you have two. Then another. Pretty soon the situation becomes unmanageable.

Hannibal, the great Carthaginian general, was attacked by a force more than three times his own in 216 B.C. The Roman general Varro had more than 72,000 men under his command. Hannibal had only 22,000. Hannibal's generals advised an immediate retreat. Instead, Hannibal took the initiative. He designed a plan that encouraged Varro to attack Hannibal's weak center while ignoring his two strong wings.

After Hannibal's center had been pushed back, the Romans were so bunched together because of his strong wings that they could not wield their swords fully. At this moment Hannibal ordered his two wings to close behind the Romans like gates. His cavalry completed the destruction. The battle developed into the most decisive in the history of warfare. More than 60,000 Romans were left dead on the field.

Note that you can take the initiative and dominate the situation even if the odds are stacked against you. Much of taking the initiative has to do with your own perception of the situation.

Lead by Example

Parachute General James Gavin jumped with his division on the D-Day invasion of Normandy. Young Colonel George S. Patton led his tanks on foot against the enemy during World War I. As a brigadier general in the same war, Douglas MacArthur went forward with the first line of his men in an attack. Major General Moshe Dayan of the Israeli Army came under direct fire while up front in an attack during the Sinai Campaign of 1956; his jeep driver was killed. Dayan was chief of staff of the Army at the time. All of these men were in take-charge situations. It was time to lead by personal example, and they did.

Few leaders in business or civilian life need to put their lives at risk or sacrifice themselves for others. Nonetheless, we can be inspired by such battlefield acts and recognize that leaders in all fields, if they really are Heroic Leaders, do lead by example, especially when taking charge in a crisis.

Flying into Fire

Colonel Jack Broughton was the chief of operations of an F-105 wing during the Vietnam War. The F-105s had a difficult mission: attack North Vietnam and especially heavily defended areas around Hanoi. It was the most heavily defended target area in the world. It was protected not only by thousands of ZPU, 23mm, 37mm, 57mm, 85mm, and 100mm anti-aircraft artillery pieces but also by numerous batteries of surface to air missiles (SAMs). Of course, there were also MiG fighters. A senior air commander normally doesn't fly all the combat missions that his crews fly. He has additional responsibilities that put demands on his time. But Jack Broughton flew all the tough ones:

> It is important that you know the people you fly with and that you know what they are doing. This does not come from sitting in an air-conditioned office and clucking

sternly over unimportant details. It comes from getting hot and sweaty and from getting your fanny shot at. There is no way to shake out people and procedures except by being a part of them. You only learn part of the game when you fly the easy ones; you have to take at least your share of the tough ones. The troops watched that schedule pretty closely. They knew who was leading for effect and who was for real, and they responded accordingly.[8]

Coast Guard to the Rescue

Douglas Munro was a signalman first class in the Coast Guard. On September 27, 1942, Signalman Munro was a petty officer in charge of twenty-four Higgins boats, a type of craft used for landing vehicles and personnel. Munro's boats were engaged in evacuating a battalion of Marines trapped by a superior number of enemy forces at Point Cruz, Guadalcanal.

Under constant fire from enemy machine guns, Signalman Munro led five of his landing craft toward the shore. The fire was so intense that he knew they would be unable to evacuate the Marines. So he positioned his own small craft, with its two guns, as a shield between the beachhead and the enemy. Naturally, he drew most of the fire in this position. His boat was hit repeatedly. But through his actions his group got the trapped Marines off the island. He saved the lives of many who otherwise would have perished. With the task nearly completed, this hero was killed by enemy fire. He was awarded posthumously the Congressional Medal of Honor.[9]

Fire and Hire

In a take-charge situation, you don't have time to fool around. You must get rid of people who are performing poorly, and you have to replace them with people who can do the job.

For most people firing is not an easy thing to do. Those you must discharge may have worked for you for some time. They may have done their best. Firing means a loss of money, prestige, security, or sense of self-worth. Still, if you are going to be true to yourself and to your organization, you may have no choice. Again, I'm not talking about ordinary day-to-day management but about take-charge situations. If your organization has a worthwhile purpose and mission, it must come first under these circumstances.

The need is easier to see in warfare, where individual acts spell the difference between life and death, victory and defeat. It is more difficult to understand in peacetime situations. What harm is it if you keep people on board who are doing a little less than they should? They may be incapable of doing any better than they already are. Ask yourself whether the crisis situation would exist if you already had fully competent performers. You will see that it is essential to get people into key positions who can do the critical job. You can't succeed with incompetents occupying these positions. Finally, you will not motivate others to go all-out in a crisis when you have demonstrated your willingness to accept less than the best from others.

Of course, simply being a leader doesn't mean you fire everyone in sight whom you think you can replace with someone better. That's not ethical, and it demonstrates poor leadership. There may well be situations below the level of a crisis when you can and should tolerate people in your organization who are not performing to your standards. An individual who is no longer capable of turning in top performance but who has done a good job in the past may be one example. Naturally, you should first attempt to save a person from being fired. You do this through counseling and the coaching techniques discussed in earlier chapters. But in a take-charge crisis, don't waste time. If someone must be fired, do it.

When Lee Iacocca turned the Chrysler Corporation around, it was the most amazing reversal in the century. Everyone said it couldn't be done. Iacocca went ahead anyway. The U.S. government guaranteed a needed loan. That helped—a lot. However, if you were to think it was just the government guarantee on a loan that made things come out, you would be dead wrong. Iacocca did it primarily with people. Like General George C. Marshall who kept notes in a safe of relatively junior officers who were potentially top leaders, Iacocca had tracked the careers of several hundred executives while at Ford Motor Company. He kept the information in a special notebook. So important was this notebook that he obtained special permission from William Ford, the president, to take the notebook with him when he went over to Chrysler. Many of the new executives he brought to Chrysler came from this notebook. You too should be directly involved with hiring executives who will work well with you.

Summary

Here are seven steps to taking charge in a crisis situation:

- Establish your objective at once. You can't lead anyone anywhere until you know where you want to go.

- Communicate what you want done until you get the attention of those you lead.

- Act boldly. This is no time to be cautious; this is a time to take risks.

- Be decisive. Don't put off making decisions.

- Dominate the situation. If you don't, the situation will dominate you.

- Lead by example. Make your motto, "Follow me," and live by it.

- Get rid of people that can't do the job, and hire people that can.

CHAPTER 23

• •

How to Develop Your Charisma

• •

Charisma comes from a Greek word meaning a divine gift. That meaning implies that charisma is something you are given; the further implication is that you receive it at birth. Napoleon Bonaparte didn't see it that way. He said, "My power is dependent upon my glory, and my glory on my victories. My power would fall if I did not base it on still more glory and still more victories. Conquest made me what I am; conquest alone can keep me there."[1]

Napoleon was saying that his being perceived as a charismatic leader was based on his success. To maintain his charisma, he had to keep being successful. There is some truth in this. Warren Bennis and Burt Nanus, two researchers from the University of Southern California, found that successful leaders tend to be viewed as charismatic.

The suggestion here is that if you want to be a charismatic leader, you must first become a successful one. I don't know about you, but I have a problem with this, even if it does contains an element of truth. What if you don't want to wait until after you are successful to be a charismatic leader? And won't being charismatic help you become a successful leader? Happily, there are actions you can take to become charismatic before you become successful.

Ronald Riggio, a social psychologist who directs the Kravis Leadership Institute at Claremont McKenna College, has developed his own methodology for creating charisma. Riggio says, "But charisma is not something that is given to a person. It is not an inherited or inborn quality. Charisma is something that develops over time. More importantly, each and every one of us has the capacity to develop our own charisma."[2]

I have observed that leaders with charisma take similar actions. This chapter outlines those actions, which you can take to develop your own charisma.

Show Your Commitment

If you want to be perceived as charismatic, it's not enough to be committed to whatever it is you are trying to accomplish. You must show your commitment to those you lead.

Several historical military leaders burned their boats after landing for an assault from the sea. Their biographers usually indicate that this was done to give their followers "no alternative." The apparent message is that they must win, since they can no longer return to the sea. I do not think that is the main reason for the action. In most cases the attacking troops could still surrender if they wished. I believe the real reason these leaders burned their boats was that it demonstrated the leader's own commitment to the goal extremely effectively.

There are many ways to demonstrate commitment, including being persistent in the pursuit of a goal, going to extraordinary lengths, self-sacrificing, risk taking, and spending personal resources. The founding fathers of the United States demonstrated commitment in all of these areas. They committed their "lives, fortunes, and sacred honor" to the goals of the group. They are generally seen as charismatic leaders.

It is hard, even impossible to show commitment if you truly aren't committed. Those you want to lead will see right through you. Commitment is something that can't be faked. Tony Alessandra, a top business and motivational speaker who has made presentations before some of America's top corporations, asks, "What do you feel passionately about? What do you care *really* deeply about? Whatever your objective—whether it's ending world hunger or ensuring better care for stray animals—you'll never influence anyone to change their ideas or take action if you don't feel strongly about it yourself."[3]

If your commitment is real, listen to Roger Ailes, who was a top media consultant to a number of CEOs and political campaigns: "The essence of charisma is showing your commitment to an idea or goal."[4] If you want to be perceived as charismatic, think of ways to show your genuine commitment.

Look the Part

Some years ago, a man did serious research on the effect of what you wear on your success on the job. The results were so astounding that his book, *Dress for Success,* became a nationwide bestseller.[5] John T. Molloy's research demonstrated conclusively that what you wear is important in becoming successful at what you do. If you are in business, you might want to pick up a copy of the book. For most jobs in the United States, Molloy's advice can be extremely valuable.

Remember that the kind of leader you are and the people you are leading can call for different types of dress. You wouldn't be perceived as being much of a charismatic leader if you tried to lead ranch hands in a business suit. In some countries businessmen and women do not dress like they do in the United States. Also, your dress should be carefully built around the image of the kind of leader you represent. The military has recognized this for a long time. Generals used to be able to design their own uniforms, and even today they dress for the image they wish to portray.

Field Marshal Bernard Montgomery was known for his special beret, on which he had fixed the emblems of the major units he commanded. He also made a pullover sweater part of his uniform. He affected a casual image, even in the heat of battle. When soldiers saw a man wearing a multi-emblem beret and casual sweater, they instantly knew him to be their commander. Patton also strongly believed in "looking the part." His special uniform consisted of a shiny helmet, pistols on both hips, and a knotted tie, even in combat! Few of his soldiers could mistake him either. Eisenhower designed the special short military jacket that he wore. Eventually, the entire U.S. Army adopted it. They called it the "Ike Jacket."

When my classmate Colonel "Tex" Turner was director of Military Instruction at West Point, he wore camouflage battle dress even in the classroom, and before the United States was at war. Tex, who formerly commanded the U.S. Army's Ranger School, is a tiger leader, and he makes sure that he looks the part. To the cadets, Tex could walk on water.

When General Alfred M. Gray was commandant of the Marine Corps, he also wore camouflage battle dress, even in the Pentagon. To my knowledge he is the only chief of staff ever to have done so in peacetime. You couldn't miss him when you saw that uniform. It said, "I am a warrior, and my Service is a fighting outfit."

You don't need to wear battle dress. But if you want charisma, you must take the time to define the image of your leader type, and then dress that way.

Dream Big

In Chapter Three I discuss why a Heroic Leader must have high expectations. I hope I demonstrated that you can achieve no higher than you expect to achieve. It is the same in setting goals for others or for a group.

Charles Garfield (the psychologist and Olympic weightlifter described in Chapter Five) observed an extraordinary leap in his own performance among engineers, workers, and production people in a major aerospace corporation that was building the Lunar Excursion Module for Apollo 11. "Every week, I heard stories about people who were lifting their performance to levels that none of them would have predicted a few months before," he said.[6] This continued during the entire period of preparing for the moon mission. On July 20, 1969, Neil Armstrong and Buzz Aldrin walked on the moon. It was over. People's performance returned to its normal level. "They had risen to a peak; then they had fallen back to earth," said Garfield.[7]

To maintain performance, the leaders of this organization should have immediately gone on to the next big dream. For as long as you ask for really big things, nothing is impossible.

At the Battle of the Bulge, the 101st Airborne Division was cut off and surrounded by superior numbers of attacking German units. Who would come to the rescue? General Patton announced that he would disengage from the enemy on one front, march a hundred miles, and be in action with three divisions within forty-eight hours. Patton knew that if it was a really important job and he demanded what was just barely possible, his men would come through.

If you want to have big dreams, you need only recall the words from the song "High Hopes," sung by Frank Sinatra. They go something like this: "You may not think that an ant can't do much with a rubber tree plant, but if he has high hopes, then Whoops! there goes another rubber tree plant!"

Tony Robbins has spoken to and changed the lives of millions of people. He has worked with many heads of state, including the president of the United States. Motivational speaker Michael Jeffreys, who wrote the bible on the subject, says, "Many people in the United States feel that Anthony Robbins is the most dynamic, most charismatic speaker on the platform today."[8] Yet Robbins is only a high school graduate; he has never been to college. What's his secret? Says Robbins, "For most of my life I've had a sense of destiny. I can remember at seven years old having images in my mind of reaching mass numbers of people and making a huge difference."[9]

Have big dreams and foster high hopes among those you lead, and your charisma will never be in doubt.

Keep Moving

Having big dreams and goals is important. But you can't let it rest at that. You must actually keep moving toward the tough goals you have set. Remember, you are the leader. People won't move until you move first. But when you do move toward a big dream, it will have a marvelous effect on those you lead. Your backers will be pleased. "What did we tell you," they'll say to others. Then there will be those who were on the fence. They supported you, but they could have gone either way. "We knew all the time that it'd work," they'll say. Finally, those who were against your big dream, who said it couldn't be done, won't say much. They'll only mutter, "Well, I'll be damned." Your charisma will increase with all concerned.

Moving toward your goals is tougher than just setting the goal, but it isn't all that hard. First, you have to have a plan. Then you set a number of intermediate goals. Every big goal has a number of smaller objectives to be accomplished first. And every objective has a number of tasks. To show movement toward the big goal, know the intermediate objectives and the tasks, and make certain those you lead know them as well. Assign each task to a specific individual along with a time when you expect that task to be accomplished. Then check periodically to see what's happening. Publicize every success, every movement toward your big goal. When those you lead run into problems, give them the help they need in order to proceed. But never stop. Whatever your goal is, maintain progress toward it.

Do Your Homework

Those who see you perform see only the effort you make on the spot. They don't see the hours and hours of homework that you have put in. Yet if you do something difficult with no apparent effort, you will be perceived as charismatic.

Doing your homework can make your reputation for a lifetime as a charismatic leader. At the Battle of Chippewa during the War of 1812, British General Phineas Riall attacked the Americans with 1,700 regulars and about 700 Indians and Canadian militia. He headed for Winfield Scott's brigade. Riall identified them as militia by their gray uniforms. He had beaten American militia and seen them break and run in previous engagements.

Winfield Scott was still a young man in his twenties. What Riall didn't know was that Scott had done his homework the previous winter. He had drilled his militia until they were ready to drop. They might have been militia, but they were now as good as regulars, or better. Under fire from Riall, they formed their line effortlessly. With parade ground precision they moved to meet Riall with bayonets.

Riall stared at the advancing Americans in amazement and uttered a tribute to Scott's abilities, which has come down through the years: "Those are regulars, By God!" Scott, who drove Riall back with heavy losses, became a general before the age of thirty, and eventually general in chief of the U.S. Army. The homework Scott did prior to the Battle of Chippewa was the original source of his success—and his charisma.

Build a Mystique

In a magic show, the magician does all sorts of wonderful tricks. The feats may be grand and involve, say, the disappearance of an elephant or the freeing of the magician after being chained in a locked trunk and lowered under tons of water. Or the tricks could involve a simple deck of cards or a few coins. The size of the trick doesn't matter; that we are fooled does. Magicians have charisma. This is because we don't understand how they are able to do their tricks, which gives them an indefinable mystique. And this is one reason why magicians never tell you how they do their tricks. They know that to do so would mean the loss of their mystique—and mystique is important to their business. If you look at leaders who are perceived to have charisma, you will see that they possess a certain mystique as well.

With magicians we know we are being fooled, but it doesn't matter. The magician knows how to do something we don't. That fact and the presentation can build an aura of mystery and be tied in to something psychologists call the "halo effect." That is, if magicians know something we don't about magic, we'll assume they know other secrets as well. This mystique can last even after the magician's death.

At the height of the interest in Japanese business success in the 1980s, American managers became aware of Miyamoto Musashi. Musashi was a seventeenth century samurai who reputedly killed more than sixty men in personal combat before he turned thirty. He was known in Japan as his country's greatest swordsman. Musashi published a small book on strategy in dueling called *The Book of Five Rings*.[10] This work had been located in Japan and later translated into English. Accompanied by scenes of Japanese art, it was published as a curio in the United States. Half in jest, someone suggested that Japanese business success was due to the principles in this book.[11] In one year, this "tabletop" book became a management best seller, selling more than one hundred thousand copies! You can still occasionally find a copy at a bookstore or order it online. The point here is that if a man who has been dead more than two hundred years can suddenly acquire a business leadership mystique, surely you and I can acquire a dose of it with a little effort.

The basic tactic is never to explain how you did something. When people are amazed that you accomplished so much in so little time, let them stay amazed. Don't explain that you were up every night for a week. Just smile. If everyone wonders how you lost twenty pounds, don't tell them you were on a diet or have been exercising. Smile. You developed a major marketing strategy in three days? So what if you were simply updating a strategy you worked out five years ago? Don't explain yourself; just smile your mysterious smile.

Please don't confuse this with another issue: you do want to keep those you lead informed. As discussed in Chapters Nine and Fourteen in the context of Direction and Persuasion, do explain to your people why you want them to do thus-and-such, if there is time. And you can explain why you did a certain thing that worked out, as part of training those who work for you. But never explain how you did something unless you are instructing, teaching, or coaching, or a subordinate is asking for help. For the routine, "Wow! How did you do that?" just smile. You'll be building your mystique.

Use the Indirect Approach

The indirect approach in strategy was developed more than two thousand years ago by a Chinese general, Sun Tzu. In this century, B. H. Liddell Hart was one of the first to realize that the indirect approach applies not only to war strategy but to a wide range of human activities, including leadership.

In his book *Strategy*, Liddell Hart said, "In all such cases, the direct assault of new ideas provokes a stubborn resistance, thus intensifying the difficulty of producing a change of outlook. . . . The indirect approach is as fundamental to the realm of politics as to the realm of sex. In commerce, the suggestion that there is a bargain to be secured is far more potent than any direct appeal to buy."[12] The indirect presentation of your ideas to others has a major advantage. It implies that you and those who receive your suggestions agree, and that there is no coercion.

Many military posts and bases require weekly inspection of the family housing areas to confirm that the lawns are being cut and the grounds cared for. But General George Marshall, chief of staff of the Army during World War II and later secretary of state, had a better way. According to Mrs. Marshall, then Colonel Marshall took command of a shabby and uncared-for post and got it fixed up without a single word of criticism. Colonel Marshall industriously cleaned and trimmed his own grounds, cut the lawn, and planted flowers. Before long, everyone on the post was out working on their own grounds, and the whole post flourished. That's setting the example, and it is also the indirect approach.[13]

To use the indirect approach, look for opportunities to get people to do things without telling them to do it directly. Look for a way that doesn't hurt the pride or self-respect of those you lead. One way to do this is simply to present the facts of the situation and let those you lead come to the obvious conclusion. When they do, give them the credit for the idea.

Summary

These are the seven actions you can take to build your charisma:

- Show your commitment.
- Look the part.
- Dream big.
- Keep moving toward your goals.
- Do your homework.
- Build a mystique.
- Use the indirect approach.

CHAPTER 24

· ·

How to Solve Problems and Make Decisions

· ·

A Heroic Leader is a decision maker and a problem solver. You can't get away from it; the two go hand in hand. Rodger D. Collons, professor of creative leadership at the American College found in his research that the ability to solve problems or contribute to problem solving is a prime characteristic of many effective leaders.[1] Confirming this recently, Ellen Weber, founder and director of MITA International Renewal Center, was asked to list the top traits a stellar leader needs. She too noted problem-solving skills as a prime requirement for good leadership.[2]

Problem-solving and decision-making skills are important for the Heroic Leader. The problems you must solve are frequently difficult and complex. Sometimes a lot is riding on your decision. Your decision making is often done under conditions of great risk and uncertainty.

The Task of All Leaders

As chairman of the Joint Chiefs of Staff, Admiral William Crowe was the highest-ranking military officer in the U.S. Armed Forces during the Reagan administration. In an interview in

Time magazine Admiral Crowe stated, "I have known individuals who made a big decision and never gave it another thought. I don't. When it's a big issue, I don't sleep soundly."[3]

Decision making under the press of combat is not unusual for commandos of any army to face. During the Gulf War, Colonel George Gray was commander of the First Special Operations Wing of the U.S. Air Force, part of the Air Commandos. Gray had a major problem. Baghdad, facing an imminent air assault, was ringed with radar stations that would give ample warning of attack. Consequently, losses in the first wave of allied aircraft were likely to be very high. The obvious solution to Gray was to have his Pave Low helicopters fly right on the desert deck and land teams of Army Green Berets on the ground to blow the radar sites up.

Colonel Gray had a problem. The politics of the situation and the risk of blowing the whole war plan were such that General Schwarzkopf wouldn't approve anybody on the ground "across the line" before H-hour. Larger aircraft had the right weapons, but the precise accuracy needed wouldn't be available. Pave Low helicopters had the electronics to find the precise targets in the darkness but were armed only with machine guns for defense. Army Apache helicopters were heavily armed but didn't have the navigation equipment needed to find the targets in the dark.

Colonel Gray came up with a solution, which he presented to General Schwarzkopf. Gray's Pave Lows would act as pathfinders for the Army Apaches, which would destroy the radar sites. Schwarzkopf liked and authorized the training and preparation for the mission. When at last they were ready, Schwarzkopf watched the rehearsal. Turning to Gray, he asked, "Can you guarantee me 100 percent?"

After a long pause, Colonel Gray responded, "Yes sir, I will."

"Okay, Colonel, you can start the war," Schwarzkopf told him.[4]

The rest is history. Even in the first wave allied losses were minimal. The successful air campaign translated into minimal losses on the ground as well, and General Schwarzkopf's total losses were only a few hundred, despite the large number of troops engaged and his resounding victory.

Keep Problems from Overcoming Your Vision

On the way to reach your goal, you are bound to come up against obstacles. Sometimes, everything that can go wrong will go wrong. That's the nature of the process in reaching any worthwhile goal. It's normal to have problems. Expect them. But as a leader, be ready to solve problems when they occur.

How can you be assured of solving problems? First you have to understand that you will encounter two types of problems. One type you usually shouldn't attempt to solve yourself. The other type, only you can solve. Let's look at both.

Problems to Delegate

Many problems you encounter should be left to others in your organization to solve. There are several reasons for this. If you become your organization's routine problem solver, you will soon find that the members of your organization will bring more and more problems to your doorstep. Soon you will be spending all your time solving problems and will have little time left for strategic planning or even general thinking. You will spend your time firefighting, and they won't even be your fires.

Another reason you shouldn't try to solve all problems yourself is that you will rob your subordinates of valuable training in problem solving. More than one leader has failed as a result of becoming the indispensable person in an organization. The inevitable time came when this leader wasn't available to solve an important problem, and subordinates dropped the brick. They either procrastinated until no solution could save the situation, or they came up with a poor solution because of their lack of training.

Finally, when those who follow you are successful in solving a problem, there is a feeling of accomplishment and an increase in self-confidence. This can enhance the overall performance of your organization in the future. When you solve all problems yourself, you deprive people of these benefits.

This doesn't mean that when there is a problem you do nothing but smile. Of course you should help those who follow you solve their problems with ideas or suggestions, if you are asked. Make it as easy as you can for them to solve their problems. But the problems should be theirs, not yours.

As General Perry M. Smith says, "By being the problem solver of last resort, the leader can help the organization grow and thrive."[5]

Problems to Keep

Some situations demand that you be the problem solver, regardless of the level at which you are operating.

E. M. Lee, president and CEO of Information Handling Services of Englewood, Colorado, puts it this way: "The CEO has to be the problem-solver. He has to be able to crack open problems, as I call it, then call on others for expertise, reduce the problem to manageable pieces," and finally develop "a framework for judgment."[6]

Here are some situations in which you must be the problem solver:

- The problem pertains to the leadership of your organization.

- You have unique expertise, knowledge, or experience required in the problem's solution.

- It is an emergency, and you have the experience and skills to solve the problem.

- Those who follow you are stuck.

Solving Problems

Effective leaders know how to solve problems. In other words, they don't dither about what they're going to do, hoping the answer will come. They have certain structured methods that they employ as tools. Depending on the problem and the situation, they select the right tool for the right job. Then they proceed. Here are three tools to help you solve your problems as a leader:

Brainstorming

Psychological techniques

Analysis of alternatives

Brainstorming

Brainstorming is a group problem-solving methodology. The basic idea is very simple. Two or more individuals get together and bounce ideas off one another. No idea, no matter how outlandish, is excluded. Ideas are built on each other, and eventually a preferred solution emerges. Two decision-making researchers, my friends Alan Rowe from the University of Southern California and Jim Boulgarides from California State University Los Angeles, have found that brainstorming forces people to think freely by removing the barriers of inhibition, self-criticism, and criticism of others. "The technique tends to generate more ideas and increases the chances of success," they say.[7]

Use brainstorming under the following conditions:

- Your group contains a lot of expertise, and you want to make use of as much of this expertise as possible.
- You want maximum commitment to the problem's solution.
- You want a really creative solution.

You are more likely to get widespread commitment with brainstorming because everyone you invite will participate in the problem solving. They will have ownership in the solution. And you'll get more creativity because in a brainstorming session you're going to really let your hair down. You'll listen to all sorts of ideas. Some will be pretty strange and unworkable. Still, the fact that you're willing to listen may dredge up some very creative ideas. I'm willing to bet that whatever solution comes out of a brainstorming session, you wouldn't have thought of it on your own.

How to Conduct a Brainstorming Session

Conducting a brainstorming session can be a real challenge. The idea is to get the most ideas you can and not to kill any ideas prematurely. You must maintain some control without dimming the enthusiasm. In an effective brainstorming session the ideas will be coming thick and fast. Find someone who can write fast and legibly on a blackboard to record the group's ideas.

First introduce the problem. State any limitations or conditions to the problem, but keep even these open to closer examination. Answer any questions about the problem that you can. Then ask for ideas for solving the problem.

Write down every idea someone suggests on the blackboard so that everyone can see it. Encourage new ideas and building on ideas that have already been suggested. This means you should constantly give recognition for suggestions as they are made. Don't allow any member of the group to criticize any ideas that are suggested, no matter how ridiculous or bizarre. Focus on how to make apparently impractical ideas work rather than on why they won't.

Wait until the group runs out of ideas, then examine the ideas for their practicality. Be ready to entertain new ideas at any time. Keep recording the main points made by the group on the blackboard. Continue to answer questions that group members may have about the problem.

Eventually, you'll narrow down the suggestions to a few solutions that appear to be promising. Focus your discussion on these until there is a consensus regarding the preferred solution.[8]

Make sure each member of your brainstorming session is aware of your appreciation for each contribution. You are still the group leader. Even though the group has come to a consensus solution to the problem, it is still your decision to adopt the decision, or whether to adopt it in some modified form. Your decision-making power in no way detracts from the fact that members made important contributions to your understanding of the problem.

Psychological Techniques

Psychological techniques have to do with using the mind. Some leaders avoid using psychological techniques. Leaders tend to be hardheaded and action oriented. The psychological tends to smell of the soft and uncertain, the touchy-feely stuff with which they may often be uncomfortable. Many of these same leaders would be surprised to learn that they have already used psychological techniques in their problem solving without realizing it.

Maybe you have. Have you ever had a problem that was bothering you, and you finally fell asleep without a solution? Chances are, when you awoke in the morning, there was the solution with no prompting. It just popped into your mind. If you thought about this outcome at all, you probably figured that your intuition had been at work.

Whether you planned to or not, you used a psychological technique in arriving at a solution. What really happened? Unsuccessful at coming up with a solution, your conscious mind eventually got tired. It had to sleep, and eventually it did. But the subconscious mind never sleeps. It is awake twenty-four hours a day, but it is in control only when your conscious mind is asleep. In our example your conscious mind went to sleep without the solution. It turned the problem over to your subconscious mind. Like a changing of the guard, your subconscious mind went to work on the problem, and it found a solution. After you woke up, it gave this solution to your conscious mind.

Famous builder, entrepreneur, and dealmaker Donald Trump can attest to the importance of this phenomenon. In his book *Trump: The Art of the Deal* he relates how a friend wanted him to invest $50 million in a "no lose" proposition. At first Trump agreed. As Trump tells it, "The papers were being drawn up, and then one morning I woke up and it just didn't feel right." Trump decided not to invest. Several months later, the company went bankrupt, and the investors lost all the money they put up.[9]

Zelma Barinov has been investigating decision making for more than twenty-five years. After finishing her doctorate in information science and cybernetics in Moscow, she headed a department at a research center. According to Barinov, 98 percent—in some cases 100 percent—of crucial decision-making information is nonverbal. She says, "Your unconscious is the most influential player on your decision team."[10]

Why the Subconscious Can Sometimes Beat the Conscious Mind

Once you have all the facts, it is not unusual for your subconscious mind to do a better job of problem solving than your conscious mind. Why is this so? One reason is that your subconscious mind has no distractions. Your conscious mind is distracted by other problems, by worry, fear, time pressure, and other elements. And your subconscious mind has more time to work on the problem. Most people can't stay still long enough to really get to work on a problem without being disturbed or having to do something else. Not so with your subconscious mind; it keeps working as long as you are asleep. Finally, your subconscious mind may not be limited by false assumptions that your conscious mind may make. For example, you may remember a certain fact incorrectly. But your subconscious mind remembers perfectly. Thus it can come to a solution your conscious mind would reject simply because of a faulty premise.

Encouraging Your Subconscious Mind

There's no question that your subconscious mind can come up with the solution to a particular problem. But if you want to use this phenomenon as a problem-solving technique, you've got to use a definite approach. I recommend the following procedure:

1. Get as much information as you can about the problem. Read everything you can find. Talk to people who may have a bearing on the solution. Investigate similar problems and how they were resolved.

2. Before you go to sleep, set aside a period of a half hour to an hour in which you do nothing but think about the problem and analyze the data you have obtained.

3. Go to sleep naturally. Do not try to force the issue. Relax and do not worry. Keep a pencil and paper by your bed; although the solution usually comes the following morning when you are awake, it may come in the middle of the night. If it does, and you are suddenly awake, write the solution down immediately. It is possible to be semi-awake and arrive at a solution in the middle of the night, only to forget it so that you don't know it in the morning.

Analysis of Alternatives

The U.S. military establishment developed the analysis of alternatives or staff study technique in the 1890s. It is an effective method for considering major factors and comparing alternative solutions. It is also useful as a means of documenting your analysis and presenting it to others. It is so popular today that many professions use it. It is taught at Harvard Business School; attorneys and some medical practitioners use it; Peter Drucker recommended it. And of course, the military still uses it. A method that has such flexibility to be of use in entirely different professions must be pretty powerful—and it is.

There are six steps to the analysis of alternatives method:

1. Define the problem's center of gravity and write the problem statement.
2. Determine the relevant factors.
3. Develop alternative solutions and think through the advantages and disadvantages of each.
4. Analyze and compare the relative merits of each alternative.
5. Draw conclusions from your analysis.
6. Choose the alternative which best solves your problem.

Many leaders have discovered that within their problems lies the key to even greater success. In the words of the successful Confederate general Nathan Bedford Forrest, "If the enemy is in our rear, then we're in his."

Earl Nightingale, the famous motivational speaker and then president of Nightingales-Conant, the largest motivational audio-tape and later CD and video company in the world, once related a story that confirms General Forrest's philosophy. The story concerned billionaire entrepreneur W. Clements Stone. Whenever his staff would come to him with a serious problem, Stone would always answer enthusiastically, "Good, excellent." He knew that the other side of any problem was a potential fortune. "Inside a problem are the keys to an even greater success," he said. In solving these, he frequently came up with ideas that made him immense sums of money. His problems were the keys to his success in making his fortune. No wonder he was enthusiastic about them.

Do not worry about your problems or the decisions you must make as a leader. Get started on turning your leadership problems into successes by using the techniques in this chapter. Become a heroic problem solver, and you will become a Heroic Leader.

Summary

If you want to solve leadership problems fast, start doing the following today:

- Separate the problems you should delegate from the ones you need to solve yourself.

- If you have problems that can best be solved by your group acting together, use brainstorming.

- For problems you must solve yourself, use a psychological technique or the analysis of alternatives.

EPILOGUE

· ·

Strong determination and perseverance in carrying through
a simple idea are the surest routes to one's objective.

—Field Marshal Helmuth Graf von Moltke

From the distant past to as far as we might see into the future, the
wisdom and principles of Heroic Leadership do not change. They are
as true today as they were in the times of the ancients, and they
will be as true thousands of years from now.

Those who put Heroic Leadership into practice will lead better and more effectively. The organizations they lead will be more
productive. There will be fewer failures, and more and greater
successes. Leaders and those who follow them will be happier
and wealthier, more content in the tasks they are engaged in and
with what they produce. Leaders practicing Heroic Leadership do
so with integrity and honor. My research on combat leaders and
civilian leaders shows this. Seven thousand years of recorded history confirm it. But in order to reap the powerful results of Heroic
Leadership, its principles must be acted on.

Why Can't Leaders Lead?

Aspects of Heroic Leadership are touched on in just about every
leadership book. They are on almost everyone's "must do" list in
one form or another. Yet though these leadership principles are
universally praised in industry, government, business, and the military, they are far too infrequently followed. Why is this so?

Heroic Leadership may be unchanging over the millennia,
but its principles are not common sense or automatic. We are not

born with knowledge of them. They may appear to be obvious if we think about them in retrospect or observe them as stand-alone commandments without thinking through their application to our own lives. But implementing them can rarely be accomplished without considerable thought, intention, and action.

The operation of complex machinery, such as driving an automobile, makes a good analogy. After we learn the basics of driving and gain a little experience, we can drive an automobile, pushing the right levers and turning the wheels at the right times. In doing this, we obey the laws of physics automatically and instinctively, without paying much thought to it. However, as driving safety experts warn us, there is danger in instinctive driving. This is because when situations that are out of the ordinary occur, we are unprepared to meet them and react too slowly. In response, safety experts exhort us to "Drive defensively." Defensive driving requires us to think. We must not drive "on automatic" but assume an active role in our driving activities. When we do this, we drive more safely and have fewer accidents.

Similarly, with experience in leading we gain proficiency and can lead almost instinctively. But beware, because leadership situations that are out of the ordinary occur every day, presenting us with unexpected challenges. We cannot lead "on automatic." Good leadership must be grounded in the principles of Heroic Leadership. Once we understand these principles, they may seem obvious, and we may even take them for granted. There lies the danger.

How else can we explain leaders who seem to ignore the principles of Heroic Leadership in practice? It may be obvious that a leader who cannot be trusted to tell the truth or do the right thing will not have loyal followers. Consciously or unconsciously, followers will analyze every situation and obey only when they perceive it to be in their best interests to do so. They will take nothing on faith from such a leader. Unfortunately, leaders of low integrity are not uncommon.

There is no question that people expect their leaders to know their stuff. Yet the shelves are filled with self-help books that focus on how to acquire power over others through trickery or manipulation rather than merit. I recall a book that recommended locating one's desk so that light would shine in the eyes of visitors. This was defined as a "power position." Nowhere did the author stress that you had to know what you were talking about, no matter how your desk was positioned.

It may seem obvious that leaders should declare their expectations. Yet many leaders keep their real intentions secret, as if revealing what they want accomplished would put some sort of curse on their intentions, or as though they would look bad in the eyes of others if they failed to attain their goal.

Why would any leaders believe that followers can be induced to be more committed than the leaders themselves? Yet some leaders pride themselves on their coolness and detachment in the pursuit of required organizational tasks, as if their attainment mattered not at all.

How can anyone succeed when he or she expects to fail? On rare occasions I suppose this happens, but it is not the norm. All the research shows that you tend to get what you expect in life. If you expect positive results, that's what you'll generally get. And if you expect the opposite, you'll generally get those, too. Yet some leaders actually begin their declarations with, "I don't think we can do this but . . ." or "I doubt you'll be able to accomplish this, but . . ." Such leaders don't expect to succeed, so they set things up to fail.

It may seem obvious that a true leader always takes care of his or her people. Yet some leaders seem to care less. They let those who follow them fend for themselves. Worse, they sometimes make a point of prioritizing their own interests above those of their followers. It is as if they believe that such a display of power somehow enhances their ability to lead. They could not be more wrong.

A leader's duty is derived from a sense of purpose or mission in life. But some leaders subvert their duty, simultaneously destroying or at least undermining their own life missions. With such incongruent behavior, is it any wonder when their followers fail to work up much enthusiasm for following, or even obeying?

When we were children playing "Follow the Leader," we lined up behind the leader we had elected. The leader then led us in a variety of feats of strength, agility, bravado, or just plain silliness. An important lesson may be found in this childhood game. The leader led from the front. Always. If the leader was not in front, he or she could not be followed. Several years ago Robert Fulghum wrote a best-selling book, *All I Really Need to Know I Learned in Kindergarten*. Clearly, there is much truth in these words. And there is no doubt that a leader can only lead by getting out in front.

The Stuff of Heroes

Applying Heroic Leadership is far from easy. It takes courage to maintain absolute integrity. It takes courage to put your career on hold while taking the time to learn your stuff. It takes courage to risk looking silly or wrong by declaring your expectations. To risk all by demonstrating absolute commitment. To expect positive results when others tell you that you are certain to fail. To protect your people from others, sometimes from your own boss. To put your duty toward your mission and your people first. To get out in front despite multiple demands on your time and exposure to what others may say and do to you. It takes courage and hard work to try, fail, and try again to follow the eight behavioral influence strategies. The leaders who do these things have earned the right to lead their organizations into the future.

Leaders who have the stuff of heroes will help us build a better, more productive future in all aspects of our lives. Who are these leaders of tomorrow? Some are already known; most are not. Some of them will achieve great fame. Others will never be well known outside of their communities, but they will be equally great. Who are the Heroic Leaders of the future? I cannot say today, but I hope and pray that one of them is you.

NOTES

Chapter One

1. Powell, Colin, *My American Journey* (New York: Random House, 1995), p. 149.
2. Jefferson, Thomas, August 19, 1775, quoted in Robert A. Fitton, ed., *Leadership: Quotations from the Military Tradition* (Boulder, CO: Westview Press, 1990), p. 297.
3. Kelly, Orr, *From a Dark Sky* (New York: Pocket Books, 1996), p. 280.
4. McCutchan, Clay, telephone conversation with author, October 1, 1997; letter to author, March 10, 1998.
5. McCall, M. W., Jr., and Lombardo, M. M., "What Makes a Top Executive?" *Psychology Today* (February 1983), pp. 26–31.
6. Poe, Richard, "A Winning Spirit—It Takes Integrity to Lead Franchises to Victory," *Success* 37:6 (August 1990), p. 60.
7. Ibid.

Chapter Two

1. National Research Council, with the Science Service, *Psychology for the Fighting Man*, 2nd ed. (New York: Penguin Books, 1944), p. 307.
2. Schwartz, William L., survey form and letter to author, May 3, 1996.
3. Fisher, Anne, "Six Ways to Supercharge Your Career," *Fortune* (January 13, 1997), p. 46.
4. Hackett, Sir John, *The Profession of Arms* (New York: Macmillan, 1983), p. 217.
5. Dupuy, R. Ernest, and Dupuy, Trevor N., *Military Heritage of America* (New York: McGraw-Hill, 1956), pp. 86–91.
6. Stuberg, Robert, "An Interview with Wayne Root," *Insight*, no. 175 (Niles, IL: Nightingale-Comnant, 1997).

7. Brodsky, Norm, "Failure Can Be the Best Teacher You'll Ever Have—Provided You're Ready to Learn," *Inc.* magazine archives, Inc. Online (November 1996), p. 31.

Chapter Three

1. Crichton, Theodore P., telephone interview with author, July 12, 1996.
2. Obama, Barack, interview by Matt Lauer, *Today Show* (NBC), January 13, 2009.
3. Mackmull, Jack V., letter to author, July 30, 1993.
4. Gaines, Charles, *Yours in Perfect Manhood, Charles Atlas* (New York: Simon and Schuster, 1982), p. 69.
5. Zlatoper, R. J., interview with the author, January 7, 1998.
6. "R. J. Zlatoper," Greater Good Television website, accessed January 16, 2009, www.greatergoodtelevision.com/guest.php?gid=5&mode=b.
7. Payne, Don H., letter to author, July 31, 1993.

Chapter Four

1. Markham, Edward, letter to author, July 27, 1993.
2. Patterson, George K., letter to author, July 26, 1993.
3. Maskaly, Michelle, Donaldson-Evans, Catherine, and Associated Press, "U.S. Airways Plane Crash-Lands in New York City's Hudson River, Everyone Survives" (Foxnews.com), January 16, 2009, accessed January 20, 2009, www.foxnews.com/story/0,2933,480078,00.html.
4. Bonaparte, Napoleon, *Maxims of Napoleon,* LXVII, originally published in Paris in 1830 and translated into English shortly thereafter; in Jomini, Clausewitz, and Schlieffen (West Point, NY: Department of Military Art and Engineering, United States Military Academy, 1954), p. 89.
5. Patterson, George K., telephone conversations with author, April 4, 11, 1996.
6. Naviaux, J., fax to author, April 9, 1996.
7. Baxter, Walter H., letter to author, August 3, 1993.
8. Tankersley, W. H., letter to author, January 1, 1993.
9. Schine, Eric, and Elstrom, Peter, "Not Exactly an Overnight Success," *Business Week* (June 2, 1997), p. 133.

10. "CDMA Technology," CDMA Development Group website, accessed January 20, 2008, www.cdg.org/technology/index.asp.

11. Qualcomm website, accessed March 30, 2005, www.qualcomm.com/about /index.html.

12. "Qualcomm 2008 Corporate Overview," p. 2, Qualcomm website, accessed January 19, 2009, http://files.shareholder.com/downloads/QCOM /522071364x0x263723/424B3FF8–2240–4912–8537–8656DFFCF267 /Qualcomm_08Overview.pdf.

Chapter Five

1. Dodd, Mathew, "The Gunfight at Takur Ghar," PTSD Support Services, January 21, 2009, accessed January 21, 2009, www.ptsdsupport.net/chief_ slabinski.html.

2. Powell, Colin L., "Colin Powell's Rules" [handout], Los Angeles Times Management Conference, March 19, 1993, Los Angeles.

3. Drucker, Peter F., *The Practice of Management* (New York: Harper and Row, 1955), p. 194.

4. Grant, Michael, *Classical Historians* (New York: Charles Scribner's Sons, 1992), p. 101.

5. Xenophon, *The Persian Expedition*, translated by Rex Warner (Baltimore: Penguin, 1949), p. 104.

6. Vandenberg, Hoyt S., Jr., letter to author, July 5, 1993.

7. "Supercuts, Inc.," Funding Universe website, accessed July 4, 2009, www.fundinguniverse.com/company-histories/Supercuts-Inc-Company-History.html.

8. Powell, Colin L., address to Los Angeles Times Management Conference, March 19, 1993, Los Angeles.

9. Garfield, Charles, *Peak Performers* (New York: Avon, 1986), pp. 71–75.

10. Leavitt, Lloyd R., letter to author, August 13, 1993.

11. Stewart, George R., *Pickett's Charge* (Greenwich, CT: Fawcett, 1963), p. 232.

Chapter Six

1. Bolte, Philip L., letter to author, September 4, 1993.

2. Noel, Thomas E., III, telephone interview with author, January 6, 1998.

3. Macartney, Jane, "China Contaminated Milk Formula Scandal Puts Babies at Risk in Other Countries" (Times Online), September 20, 2008, accessed January 29, 2009, www.timesonline.co.uk/tol/news/world/asia /article4790866.ece.

4. Harris, Gardiner, "Salmonella Was Found at Peanut Plant Before," *New York Times*, January 28, 2009, accessed January 29, 2009, www.nytimes.com/2009/01/28/us/29Peanut.html?ref=dining.

5. Burgess, Lisa, "I Started Patching Them Up Real Quick," *Stars and Stripes*, June 14, 2005, accessed July 4, 2009, www.stripes.com/article.asp?section=104&article=28897&archive=true.

6. Whitmore, David, interview with author, November 8, 1997.

7. Summers, Harry G., "Take Care of the Troops," *Washington Times*, August 7, 1997, p. 14.

8. Ibid.

9. Broughton, Jack, *Going Downtown* (New York: Orion Books, 1988), p. 218.

10. Broughton, Jack, telephone interviews with author, December 4, 8, 1997.

Chapter Seven

1. Schwarzkopf, H. Norman, *It Doesn't Take a Hero* (New York: Bantam, 1992), p. 148.

2. Walters, Harry N., telephone interview with author, January 12, 1998.

3. Sloan, Allan, "The Hit Men," *Newsweek* (February 26, 1996), pp. 44–48.

4. Blake, Robert R., and Mouton, Jane S., *The New Managerial Grid* (Houston: Gulf, 1964, 1978), p. 95.

5. Ross, Scott, "Merrill Boss Canned from Million Dollar Office" (Washington News), January 23, 2009, accessed January 30, 2009, www.nbcwashington.com/news/business/Merrill-Boss-Canned.html.

6. Keegan, John, *The Mask of Command* (New York: Penguin, 1988), p. 46.

7. Ibid.

8. Iverson, Ken, *Plain Talk* (New York: John Wiley & Sons, 1998), p. 13.

9. Iverson, Ken, letter to author, October 21, 1997.

10. Iverson, Ken, telephone interview with author, October 30, 1997. For a quick general history of the company, see the Wikipedia entry, http://en.wikipedia.org/wiki/Nucor.

Chapter Eight

1. Aderholt, Harry C., letter to author, September 7, 1993.

2. Mack, Toni, "Indiana Jones, Meet Mark Chandler," *Forbes* (May 23, 1994), pp. 100–104.

3. "Biophysical Management Team," Biophysical website, accessed February 1, 2009, www.biophysicalcorp.com/about-us/management-team.aspx.

4. Nutting, Wallace H., letter to author, September 13, 1996.

5. Keegan, John, *The Mask of Command* (New York: Penguin, 1988), p. 329.

6. Bongiorno, Lor, "'The McDonald's of Toiletries,'" *Business Week* (August 4, 1997), pp. 79–80.

7. "Beth M. Prichard," Forbes website, accessed February 1, 2009, http://people.forbes.com/profile/beth-m-pritchard/28320.

8. "Jodie Glore Selected as 2007 Distinguished Alum," Association of Graduates, USMA, website, April 2007, accessed January 29, 2009, www.aogusma.org/as/firstcall/apr07/jodieglore.htm.

9. Glore, Jodie K., telephone interview with author, January 9, 1998.

10. Glasner, Connie, "Get Comfortable in Your Own Management Skin" (BizJournals), accessed February 1, 2009, www.connieglaser.com/article-archives/management_skin.html.

11. Burrows, Peter, "The Man in the Disk Driver's Seat," *Business Week* (March 18, 1996), p. 71.

12. Ibid., p.72.

13. Markoff, John, "Alan F. Shugart, 76, a Developer of Disk Drive Industry, Dies," *New York Times*, December 15, 2006, accessed February 1, 2009, www.nytimes.com/2006/12/15/obituaries/15shugart.html.

Chapter Nine

1. Dodd, Matthew, "Coffman's Commandos," *Defense Watch*, July 5, 2007, accessed February 14, 2009, www.sftt.org/cgi-bin/csNews/csnews.cgi/csNews.cgi?database=DefenseWatch 2007.db&command=viewone&op=t&id=178&rnd=293.99304438112193.

2. Glasier, Connie, and Smalley, Barbara Steinberg, *Swim with the Dolphins* (New York: Warner Books, 1995), pp. 12–17; Holusha, John, "Grace Pastiak's 'Web of Inclusion,'" *New York Times*, Business Section, May 5, 1991, accessed January 19, 2009, http://query.nytimes.com/gst/fullpage.html?res=9D0CE4D91131F936A35756C0A967958260.

Chapter Ten

1. Malek, Frederic V., letter to author, December 8, 1997.

2. Malek, Frederic V., telephone interview with author, January 21, 1998, and fax, January 22, 1998; "Companies: Thayer/Hidden Creek," *Business Week*, accessed February 13, 2009, http://investing.businessweek.com/research/stocks/private/snapshot.asp?privcapId=23309.

3. Powell, Colin L., with Persico, Joseph E., *My American Journey* (New York: Random House, 1995), p. 167.

4. Ibid.

5. Ibid.

6. Trump, Donald J., and Schwartz, Tony, *Trump: The Art of the Deal* (New York: Warner Books, 1987), p. 140.

7. "James Clavell," Wikipedia entry, accessed February 12, 2009, http://en.wikipedia.org/wiki/James_Clavell.

8. Abrashoff, D. Michael, "Building Up Your People," *Public Management*, 86 (October 2004), accessed February 14, 2009, www.icma.org/pm/8609/public/abrashoff.cfm.

Chapter Eleven

1. Harris, Shane, "2004 Service to America Medals: Career Achievement Courage in Crisis," Government Executive.com, October 1, 2004, accessed February 20, 2009, www.govexec.com/features/1004sam/1004samS2.htm.

2. *The Armed Forces Officer* (Washington, DC: U.S. Government Printing Office, 1950), p. 86.

3. "Colonel Chamberlain and the 20th Maine Infantry," National Park Service website, Voices of Battle, accessed July 5, 2009, www.nps.gov/archive/gett/getttour/sidebar/chambln.htm.

Chapter Twelve

1. "Pershing," The Leaders, accessed July 5, 2009, www.diggerhistory.info/pages-leaders/ww1/pershing.htm.

2. Munch, Paul G., "General George C. Marshall and the Army Staff," March 19, 1992, p. 5, accessed July 6, 2009, www.au.af.mil/au/awc/awcgate/army/p081.pdf.

3. AFM 35–15, *Air Force Leadership* (Washington, DC: Department of the Air Force, 1948), p. 33.

Chapter Thirteen

1. Cialdini, Robert B., *The Psychology of Influence*, rev. ed. (New York: William Morrow, 1993), p. 4.

2. Boyington, Gregory, *Baa Baa Black Sheep* (New York: Bantam Books, 1977), p. 185.

Chapter Fourteen

1. "Vice-Admiral Harry DeWolf: A Canadian Naval Legend," Friends of HMCS Haida website, September 20, 1999, accessed September 3, 2009, http://hmcshaida.ca/dewolf.html.

Chapter Fifteen

1. Selig, Robert A., "Francois Joseph Paul Compte de Grasse, the Battle Off the Virginia Capes, and the American Victory at Yorktown," accessed July 5, 2009, www.americanrevolution.org/degrasse.html.

2. MacArthur, Douglas, *Reminiscences* (New York: McGraw-Hill, 1964), p. 70.

Chapter Sixteen

1. Cumings, Pamela C., *The Power Handbook* (Boston: CBI Publishing, 1981), p. 100.

Chapter Seventeen

1. Mapp, Alf J., Jr., *Frock Coats and Epaulets* (New York: Hamilton Press, 1987), p. 203.

2. Puryear, Edgar F., Jr., *Nineteen Stars: A Study in Military Character and Leadership* (Presidio, CA: Presidio Press, 1971), p. 149.

3. Mendleson, Jack L., "Manager Disrespect," *Business Forum* (Winter/Spring 1998), p. 20.

4. Hammonds, Keith H., "Balancing Work and Family," *Business Week* (September 16, 1996), p. 74.

5. "Awards," First Horizon National Corporation website, accessed June 12, 2009, www.fhnc.com/index.cfm?Fuseaction=Newsroom.Awards.

6. Dodd, Mathew, "A Hero Who Walked His Talk," Soldiers for the Truth, February 7, 2007, accessed June 15, 2009, www.sftt.org/cgi-bin/csNews/csnews.cgi?csNews.cgi?database=DefenseWatch 2007. db&command=viewone&op=t&id=146&rnd=467.2264312980463.

7. Johnson, Martin L., "A True Leader," After Hours Inspirational Stories, accessed June 12, 2009, www.inspirationalstories.com/8/836.html.

8. Blanchard, Kenneth, and Johnson, Spencer, *The One Minute Manager* (New York: William Morrow, 1982).

9. Puryear, *Nineteen Stars*, pp. 229–230.

10. Linowes, Jonathan, "MBWA, Management by Wandering Around," *Natural Entrepreneur*, June 12, 2009, accessed June 12, 2009, www.nenh .com/articles/20040908–03.html.

11. Patton, George S., quoted in Alan Axelrod, *Patton on Leadership* (New York: Prentice Hall, 1999), p. 102.

Chapter Eighteen

1. "Building Self-Confidence," Mind Tools website, accessed June 15, 2009, www.mindtools.com/selfconf.html.

2. AFM 35–15, *Air Force Leadership* (Washington, DC: Department of the Air Force, 1948), p. 30.

3. Schwarzenegger, Arnold, with Hall, Douglas Kent, *Arnold: The Education of a Bodybuilder* (New York: Fireside, 1997), p. 24.

4. Garfield, Charles, *Peak Performers* (New York: Avon Books, 1986), pp. 72–73.

Chapter Nineteen

1. Rodgers, Thomas, "Scouting: After Six Years a Soccer Defeat," *New York Times*, May 17, 1984, accessed June 17, 2009, www.nytimes. com/1984/05/17/sports/scouting-after-6-years-a-soccer-defeat.html.

2. Blades, Jon W., *Rules for Leadership* (Washington, DC: National Defense University, 1986), p. 75.

3. Ibid., pp. 76–78.

4. Michalisin, Michael D., Karau, Steven J., and Tangpong, Charnchai, "Leadership's Activation of Team Cohesion as a Strategic Asset: An Empirical Simulation," *Journal of Business Strategies* (Spring 2007), published in Entrepreneur Network, accessed June 17, 2009, www.entrepreneur.com/tradejournals/article/165017894.html.

5. Blades, *Rules for Leadership,* p. 100.

6. Drucker, Peter F., *The Effective Executive* (New York: Harper and Row, 1967), pp. 68–69.

7. General Patton's D-Day speech, June 5, 1944, accessed June 17, 2009, www.5ad.org/Patton_speech.htm.

Chapter Twenty

1. Puryear, Edgar F., Jr., *Nineteen Stars: A Study in Military Character and Leadership* (Presidio, CA: Presidio Press, 1971), p. 233.

2. *The Armed Forces Officer* (Washington, DC: Armed Forces Information Service, 1975), p.138.

3. "Shoot House Refines Close-Quarters Maneuvers for ERB Trainees (Baghdad)," Operation Iraqi Freedom, official website of the Multi-National Force, November 16, 2008, accessed November 19, 2009, www.mnf-iraq.com/index.php?option=com_content&task=view&id=23707&Itemid=132.

4. *Armed Forces Officer,* p. 159.

5. Cronin, Thomas E., "Thinking About Leadership," in Robert L. Taylor and William E. Rosenbach, eds., *Military Leadership* (Boulder, CO: Westview Press, 1984), p. 206.

6. Smith, Perry M., *Taking Charge* (Washington, DC: National Defense University, 1986), pp. 28–29.

7. Oliver, Dave, Jr., *Lead On!* (Novato, CA: Presidio Press, 1992), p. 147.

8. Puryear, *Nineteen Stars*, p. 326.

9. Carrison, Dan, and Walsh, Rod, *Semper Fi* (New York: AMACOM, 1999), p. 98.

Chapter Twenty-One

1. Naisbitt, John, and Auberdene, Patricia, *Re-inventing the Corporation* (New York: Warner Books, 1985), pp. 85–86.

2. Clark, Don, "Motivation Activity," March 28, 2000, accessed June 21, 2009, www.nwlink.com/~donclark/leader/want_job.html.

3. Drucker, Peter F., *Management Challenges of the 21st Century* (New York: Harper Business, 1999), pp. 20–21.

4. Baffin, John, *Links of Leadership* (New York: Abelard-Schuman, 1970), p. 189.

5. Ibid.

6. Burns, James MacGregor, *Leadership* (New York: Harper and Row, 1978).

7. Burns, James MacGregor, quoted in William Safire and Leonard Safer, *Leadership* (New York: Simon and Schuster, 1990), p. 202.

8. Hilton, Warren, *Applied Psychology: Processes and Personality* (San Francisco: Applied Psychology Press, 1920), p. 97.

9. Podesta, Connie, and Gatz, Jean, *How to Be the Person Successful Companies Fight to Keep* (New York: Simon and Schuster, 1997), p. 184.

10. Nelson, Bob, *1001 Ways to Reward Employees* (New York: Workman Press, 1994).

11. "Asch's New Boss, Gen. Randolph," *Airman* (December 1987), p. 9.

12. Burger, Chester, *The Chief Executive* (Boston: CBI Publishing, 1978), p. 48.

13. "2008 Annual Report," McCormick & Company, accessed June 22, 2009, http://media.corporate-ir.net/media_files/irol/65/65454/reports /IR_AR2008/01.html.

14. Burger, *The Chief Executive*, p. 24.

Chapter Twenty-Two

1. Montgomery, Bernard Law, *Montgomery of Alamein, The Memoirs of Field-Marshal Montgomery* (New York: World Publishing, 1958), p. 94.

2. Ibid., p. 93.

3. Ibid., p. 75.

4. Williamson, Porter B., *Patton's Principles* (New York: Simon and Schuster, 1979), p. 31.

5. Patton, George S., *War As I Knew It* (New York: Pyramid, 1966), p. 309.

6. Patton, *War As I Knew It*, p. 308.

7. Kotter, John P., *Matsushita on Leadership* (New York: Free Press, 1997), p. 10.

8. Broughton, Jack, *Thud Ridge* (New York: J. B. Lippincott, 1969), p. 30.

9. Reegan, W. Richard, "Douglas A. Munro: The U.S. Coast Guard's Medal of Honor Recipient" (AC Associated News), January 9, 2006, accessed July 8, 2009, www.associatedcontent.com/article/16529/douglas_a_munro_the_us_coast_guards.html.

Chapter Twenty-Three

1. Wareham, John, *Secrets of a Corporate Headhunter* (New York: Atheneum, 1980), p. 35.

2. Riggio, Ronald E., *The Charisma Quotient* (New York: Dodd, Mead, 1987), p. 4.

3. Alessandra, Tony, *Charisma* (New York: Warner Books, 1998), p. 235.

4. Ailes, Roger, "The Secret of Charisma," *Success* (July/August, 1988), p. 14.

5. Molloy, John T., *Dress for Success* (New York: Warner Books, 1980).

6. Garfield, Charles, *Peak Performers* (New York: Avon, 1986), p. 23.

7. Ibid., p. 26.

8. Jeffreys, Michael, *Success Secrets of the Motivational Superstars* (Rocklin, CA: Prima, 1996), p. 2.

9. Ibid., p. 1.

10. Leung, Kenneth, "Kenshi, Miyamoto Musashi," June 27, 1997, accessed January 19, 2010, http://reocities.com/Colosseum/1705/musashi.html.

11. Hurst, G. Cameron, III, "Samurai on Wall Street: Miyamoto Musashi and the Search for Success," *InYo: The Journal of Alternative Perspectives on the Martial Arts and Sciences* (2001), accessed June 22, 2009, http://ejmas.com/jalt/jaltart_Hurst_0101.htm.

12. Hart, B.H. Liddell, *Strategy*, rev. ed. (New York: Frederick A. Praeger, 1962), p. 18.

13. AFM-35–15, *Air Force Leadership* (Washington, DC: Department of the Air Force, 1948), p. 45.

Chapter Twenty-Four

1. Collons, Rodger D., "Spotlight on Leadership Traits," in A. Dale Timpe, ed., *Leadership* (New York: Facts on File Publications, 1987), p. 30.

2. Weber, Ellen, "Top 5 Traits for 2008 Leaders," Brain Based Business, January 13, 2008, accessed June 22, 2009, www.brainbasedbusiness.com/2008/01/top_5_traits_for_2008_leaders.html.

3. van Voorst, Bruce, "Of War and Politics," *Time* (December 26, 1988), p. 74.

4. Kelly, Orr, *From a Dark Sky: The Story of U.S. Air Force Special Operations* (New York: Pocket Books, 1996), pp. 294–296.

5. Smith, Perry M., *Taking Charge* (Washington, DC: National Defense University Press, 1986), p. 5.

6. Day, Charles R., Jr., "What It Takes to Be a CEO," in A. Dale Timpe, ed., *Leadership* (New York: Facts on File Publications, 1987), p. 9.

7. Rowe, Alan J., and Boulgarides, James D., *Managerial Decision Making* (New York: Macmillan, 1992), p. 123.

8. "What Is Brainstorming?" Brainstorming website, accessed June 25, 2009, www.brainstorming.co.uk/tutorials/whatisbrainstorming.html.

9. Trump, Donald J., and Schwartz, Tony, *The Art of the Deal* (New York: Warner Books, 1987), pp. 27–28.

10. Barinov, Zelma, *Instant Decisions* (Bala Cynwyd, PA: Access Press, 1998), pp. 17, 154.

ABOUT THE AUTHOR

William Cohen is president of the Institute of Leader Arts (www.stuffofheroes.com) and vice president of the Peter F. Drucker Academies of China and Hong Kong. Executives and managers from more than fifty countries have heard him at speaking engagements, and at his workshops. He has taught in the graduate schools of California State University Los Angeles, the University of Southern California, TUI University, and the Peter Drucker and Masatoshi Ito Graduate School of Management at Claremont Graduate University. His books, including *Drucker on Leadership*, *A Class with Drucker*, *The New Art of the Leader*, *The Stuff of Heroes*, and *The Art of the Strategist*, have been translated into twenty-one languages.

Cohen is a retired major general from the U.S. Air Force Reserve. He has held executive positions in several companies and was president of two private universities. In addition to his B.S. in engineering from the U.S. Military Academy at West Point, he has an M.B.A. from the University of Chicago and an M.A. and Ph.D. in management from Claremont Graduate University. He is also a distinguished graduate-in-residence at the Industrial College of the Armed Forces in Washington, D.C.

Cohen's awards include the Outstanding Professor's Award at California State University Los Angeles (1982), the Freedoms Foundation of Valley Forge George Washington Honor Medal for Excellence in Economic Education (1985), and the California State University Los Angeles Statewide Outstanding Professor Award (1996). In 1999 he was named one of four "Great Teachers in Marketing" by the Academy of Marketing Science among nominees from around the world. In 2002 he received an honorary doctorate in humane letters from the International Academy for Integration of Science and Business in Moscow, Russia. Cohen was the 2006 Goolsby Distinguished Visiting Professor in Leadership at the College of Business Administration at the University of Texas at Arlington. He is the recipient of the 2009 Distinguished Alumnus Service Award from Claremont Graduate University. His military awards include the Distinguished Service Medal, the Legion of Merit, the Distinguished Flying Cross with three Oak Leaf Clusters, and many others. Cohen has served on various city, state, national, corporate, and trade boards and boards of directors.

INDEX